Teaching for Creativity in the Common Core Classroom

D1248236

Teaching for Creativity in the Common Core Classroom

Ronald A. Beghetto
James C. Kaufman
John Baer

Foreword by Robert J. Sternberg

WAGGONER LIBRARY
DISCARD

TEACHERS COLLEGE PRESS

Teachers College
Columbia University
New York and London

WAGGONER LIBRARY
TREVECCA NAZARENE UNIVERSITY

Published by Teachers College Press, 1234 Amsterdam Avenue, New York, NY
10027

Copyright © 2015 by Teachers College, Columbia University

All rights reserved. No part of this publication may be reproduced or transmitted
in any form or by any means, electronic or mechanical, including photocopy,
or any information storage and retrieval system, without permission from the
publisher.

Library of Congress Cataloging-in-Publication Data

Beghetto, Ronald A., 1969–
 Teaching for creativity in the common core classroom / Ronald A. Beghetto,
 James C. Kaufman, John Baer.
  pages cm
 Includes bibliographical references and index.
 ISBN 978-0-8077-5615-7 (pbk. : alk. paper) —
 ISBN 978-0-8077-5616-4 (hardcover : alk. paper) —
 ISBN 978-0-8077-7350-5 (ebook)
  1. Creative ability—Study and teaching. 2. Creative thinking—Study and
 teaching. 3. Education—Standards—United States. I. Kaufman, James C. II.
 Baer, John. III. Title.
 LB1590.5.B44 2015
 370.15'7--dc23   2014029633

ISBN 978-0-8077-5615-7 (paper)
ISBN 978-0-8077-5616-4 (hardcover)
ISBN 978-0-8077-7350-5 (ebook)

Printed on acid-free paper
Manufactured in the United States of America

22 21 20 19 18 17 16 15   8 7 6 5 4 3 2 1

For my sister, Christina Beghetto Miller, and mother-in-law, Kathy Lynn Walsh, two of the best teachers I know
—RAB

For Jacob Levi Kaufman and Asher Jonathan Kaufman with all of my love, forever
Dad/Daddy
—JCK

To Sylvia
—JB

Contents

Foreword Robert J. Sternberg   xi

Acknowledgments   xiii

Introduction   1

1. **Creativity and the Common Core**   8

    Vignette 1: Should Teachers Establish a Separate
    "Creativity Time" in Their Curriculum?   8

    Vignette 2: Is Creativity Really Compatible
    with Standards-Based Teaching?   8

    Common Beliefs About Creativity   9

    Common Beliefs About Content Standards   10

    Content Standards and Creativity:
    Irreconcilable Differences?   12

    Concluding Thoughts   17

    From Concepts to Classroom   18

2. **Understanding Creativity in the Classroom:**
    Getting Beyond Hidden Beliefs and Misconceptions   20

    Vignette 1: Must We Limit Originality with Cold Facts?   20

    Vignette 2: Is It Ever Okay to Stifle Creativity?   20

    Creativity: A Brief Theoretical Overview   21

    Creativity: Applying the Theories   29

    Creativity: Misperceptions   31

Creative Metacognition   32

From Concepts to Classroom   35

Concluding Thoughts   36

3. **Learning Environments that Support Creativity
   and the Common Core**   **38**

Vignette 1: Math Motorcycles   38

Vignette 2: Reading Ratatouille   39

Establishing a Supportive Learning Environment   39

From Concepts to Classroom   46

Concluding Thoughts   52

4. **Practical Applications 1:
   Creative Lessons and Insights in English and Language Arts**   **55**

Vignette 1: Meanings of Words in Various Contexts   55

Vignette 2: Writing Dialogue and Writing Creatively   56

*Vignette 3: Divergent Thinking During Character
Brainstorming and Comparison*   60

*Vignette 4: Distinguishing Among Fact, Opinion,
and Reasoned Judgment*   63

Vignette 5: Verb Tense and Student Storytelling   65

How to Teach for Creativity While Teaching the
English Language Arts (ELA) Common Core   67

From Concepts to Classroom   76

Concluding Thoughts   78

5. **Practical Applications 2:
   Creative Lessons and Insights in Mathematics**   **79**

Vignette 1: Mathematical Permutations and Combinations   79

Vignette 2: Applying Mathematical Knowledge in New Situations   81

Vignette 3: Using Design Challenges in Mathematics Teaching   85

How to Teach for Creativity While Teaching the
Mathematics Common Core   87

Concluding Thoughts   93

From Concepts to Classroom   94

6. **Where Do We Go from Here?**   **98**

What Are the Best Instructional Techniques for
Promoting Creativity?   99

Creativity Across the Curriculum   100

Assessing Creativity and Common Core Learning   102

Synthesis of Key Concepts and Tips   106

Resources for Learning More About Creativity   107

References   **111**

Index   **119**

About the Authors   **127**

Foreword

Beghetto, Kaufman, and Baer have written a path-breaking, even a revolutionary, book. Why? Because almost every serious educator has seen governmental efforts to regulate or even to guide education as creativity-killers, not as promoters of creativity. For most educators, the idea that the Common Core, or any other set of state- or federally recommended standards might be used to promote creativity seems almost oxymoronic.

This idea notwithstanding, the authors have shown in a compelling and sophisticated way how teachers can use the Common Core to promote rather than to discourage creativity. I've been in the field of education for more years than I care to count, and before I read this book, it would not even have occurred to me that such standards could be used to promote the teaching of creativity. Beghetto, Kaufman, and Baer have demonstrated their own creativity in showing how creativity and the Common Core can be compatible rather than essentially contradictory.

The Common Core standards have many opponents. Many of those opposed to them are motivated by ideology. Nothing that these authors or any other authors write will convince them otherwise. But there will be other educators who will continue to believe that the Common Core is a creativity killer. And indeed, no one could say that the standards were written specifically to promote creativity. This book discusses how creativity can be taught, *even if* Common Core standards are implemented.

Unfortunately, very few implementers of the Common Core, even those who read this wonderful book, will teach the Common Core in a way that promotes creativity. Why? I believe there are several issues our society needs to address before teaching for creativity becomes widespread.

First, we need to believe in teaching for creativity. As a society, we may say we do, but to many educators, teaching for creativity means educating students to be flexible thinkers within a fairly rigid educational framework. As long as students stay within a small circle, they are welcome to be creative.

Second, very few standardized tests make any provision for, or even encourage in the slightest way, creative thinking of the kinds the authors in this book discuss. In the United States, testing has come to drive instruction rather than instruction driving testing, so until testing changes, teaching likely won't.

Third, many teachers never learn how to teach for creativity. They may like the idea of teaching for creativity in the abstract. But they don't really know how to do it in practice.

Fourth, some educators mistakenly believe that creativity is something students display only in the arts. On this view, creativity is something you do in a class on drawing or painting. Even some educators with a broader view would draw the line at mathematics or science. But such a view of creativity is both limited and limiting, and fails to take into account that creativity can be encouraged and displayed in any field. For example, great mathematicians and scientists differ in many ways, but one thing they all have in common is extraordinary creativity.

Fifth, many educators view teaching for creativity as something you do after you have taught the basic facts, rather than a means to help students learn those basic facts. On this view, creative thinking may be promoted in some future course—a course that never occurs.

Finally, many teachers fear creative students, even though they might not admit this to others—or to themselves. Creative students are hard to teach, sometimes oppose the teacher's point of view, and sometimes question why they are even doing what they are doing. How much easier it is to have students who just do what they are told without making waves!

In sum, you are about to embark on reading a wonderful book. The book may even change the way you teach and assess your students. There are few favors you can do your students greater than putting into practice the precepts of this book. Give it a try. I will!

—Robert J. Sternberg
Professor of Human Development
Cornell University
09/20/14

Acknowledgments

We would especially like to thank Anna Dilley for her extensive work in preparing the manuscript for final submission. We are also very grateful to Allison B. Kaufman and Beth Leibson for their editorial help and insight on an earlier version of the manuscript. We would also like to thank our acquisitions editor Emily Spangler and everyone at Teacher's College Press, particularly their freelance developer Sarah Biondello.

We are grateful to our universities and departments for giving us the freedom that allows us to write these types of books. Ron and James, both new to the University of Connecticut, would like to thank their colleagues as they start this new journey. The chance to work together at the Neag School of Education alongside our dear friend and collaborator Jonathan Plucker is an amazing opportunity. We have been welcomed with open arms by everyone at UConn—President Susan Herbst, Provost Mun Choi, Vice Provost Sally Reis, outgoing dean Tom DeFranco, incoming dean Richard Schwab, department head Del Siegle, program coordinators Scott Brown and Catherine Little, and the legendary Joe Renzulli. It is an exciting time for us!

Ron would like to thank his wife, Jeralynn, and daughter Olivia for the daily inspiration and support they provide.

James would like to thank, as always, his wife, Allison, sons Jacob and Asher, and parents, Alan and Nadeen.

Introduction

The test of a first-rate intelligence is the ability to hold two opposed ideas in mind at the same time and still retain the ability to function.

—F. Scott Fitzgerald

Creativity and the Common Core State Standards Initiative (CCSSI) may seem to be an example of Fitzgerald's two opposing ideas—creativity is often described as thinking outside the box, and the Common Core could be thought of as the box itself. In this book, our goal is to show how these two seemingly opposed ideas cannot only coexist but can enrich each other.

Creativity is a hot topic today. It is listed as one of the essential 21st-century skills and widely acknowledged by schools, organizations, and leaders as vital to individual and organizational success (Beghetto & Kaufman, 2013; Kaufman, 2009). Despite creativity's recognized potential, many teachers and administrators are not quite sure what exactly it is, how it can be taught and nurtured, and whether it is even possible to assess.

The Common Core State Standards (CCSS), meanwhile, represent the latest effort to better prepare all students for entrance into postsecondary education and the workforce, outlining a common roadmap of what concepts students need to learn, regardless of their geographic location. Yet, despite the fact that the Common Core initiative was spearheaded by the National Governors Association Center for Best Practices (NGACBP) and the Council of Chief State School Officers (CCSSO), it has become a political point of contention (Bidwell, 2014), raised questions about content coverage (Porter, McMaken, Hwang, & Yang, 2011), and led to concerns about implementation and assessment—even from supporters (AFT, 2013; Strauss, 2013).

Despite these concerns, the adoption of the Common Core is moving forward. At present, 44 states (plus Washington, DC, and four U.S. territories) have adopted the Common Core State Standards ("Standards in Your State," 2014). Creativity has not been forgotten; policymakers and educational leaders continue to emphasize the need for introducing creativity into the curriculum. Both creativity and the CCSSI are of fundamental importance to education. Nurturing all students' creative potential while simultaneously providing them with a consistently high-quality education has long-term economic, cultural, and global implications. But as this debate between emphasizing CCSSI and emphasizing creativity continues, how are classroom teachers expected to keep up?

Many teachers may find themselves at a crossroads—feeling they must choose between either nurturing student creativity and conforming to common standards. Sometimes teachers feel caught between valuing both creativity and the CCSS, but the idea of combining the two seems to fly in the face of logic. How can creativity, often called uncommon and original, be combined with the CCSS, something that by definition is common and convergent? Consider a teacher who is interested in cultivating student creativity, but also sees value in the Common Core. This teacher may agree with opponents of CCSS who have raised concerns that standards-based schooling is killing student creativity (Berliner, 2011). Like No Child Left Behind before it, the Common Core State Standards Initiative brings many standardized tests. These test scores can determine the future not only of the students but also of the teachers and administrators. There is only so much time in a school day. With CCSS taking the lion's share of the time, attention, and resources of schools, creativity can seem like one more piece to be crammed into an already overcrowded curriculum.

On the other hand, that same teacher may also see inherent value in the notion that the Common Core helps ensure that all students can enjoy access to a quality education that is consistent across participating states. The teacher may agree that consistent standards are one of the few tools out there that enable education to be equitable for all students.

Indeed, the Common Core will help promote shared learning expectations for students regardless of their past school experiences. It decreases uncertainty about which concepts have already been introduced to students in previous grades or which concepts they will face in subsequent grades. The Common Core can, therefore, be a welcome means for providing guidelines for curricular content and limiting uncertainty.

The idea of introducing creativity into the curriculum may be viewed as competing with the potential benefits of the Common Core. Creativity can potentially be seen as both a source of classroom uncertainty and a poor use of time that could instead be focused on helping a diverse population attain these new, shared content standards.

Most readers of this book value helping students develop their creative thinking skills, so we will only briefly highlight the importance of teaching for creativity. Some such defenses, though well-intentioned, can use the wrong arguments. For example, one common refrain is that we need creativity to grow our economy. Although it is true that creative workers will boost the economy, using this point as a primary selling point leaves one vulnerable to critics who argue that creative writing programs probably won't grow the Gross Domestic Product (GDP) and should, therefore, be scrapped.

We believe that creativity is a good thing, both unto itself and for the myriad of positive attributes associated with it. As we have elaborated elsewhere (Kaufman & Baer, 2005; Kaufman & Beghetto, 2009, 2013a, 2013b), creative people tend to respond better to trauma and stressful situations, be in a happier mood, advance higher in their jobs, and generally are more likely to succeed. Creativity can also be used in the service of malevolent deeds (Cropley, Kaufman, & Cropley, 2008) in ways that can range from terrorists who use creative means to destroy things to criminals who use creative techniques to con people out of money (Cropley, Cropley, Kaufman, & Runco, 2010). However, we believe creativity is primarily a benevolent concept that brings good to the world and our individual lives.

We take it as a given that creativity is something teachers want to promote, just as we take it as a given that the CCSSI will guide much of what happens in classrooms across the country for many years. This book is about how to reconcile those two givens. Creativity matters; so do the CCSSI. What does that mean for teachers?

First and foremost, the CCSSI does not mean abandoning creativity. Creativity and the Common Core are not in opposition, as we will explain in more detail below. There are many ways that teaching to promote creativity and teaching the CCSSI can go together and support one another. The synergies between creativity and the Common Core far outnumber the unavoidable conflicts, but those synergies, those opportunities, are sometimes far from obvious. The twin goals of this book are (1) to help teachers see (and understand how to use) those opportunities and (2) to help teachers resolve the occasional conflicts that will inevitably arise when trying to emphasize both creativity and the Common Core.

The CCSSI carries new possibilities and new challenges. Teachers who value creativity will *not* experience more problems in the classroom because of the Common Core. Indeed, as we will argue in this book, teachers who value creativity will have extra tools at their disposal in teaching the Common Core. The tools are already there and ready to be deployed in many teachers' toolkits. Let us show you how to use them productively to promote both creativity and the Common Core.

Does the adoption of the Common Core State Standards mean that developing students' creativity has become an untenable or unrealistic objective? Are the goals of developing students' creativity and meeting specific content standards at odds? We don't have sufficient empirical evidence to properly answer these questions. But we do believe that the accumulated indirect evidence is compelling. The answer to these questions seems to be, as is so often the case in education, "It depends." Sometimes there is a conflict between promoting creativity and promoting the acquisition of skills and content knowledge, and it is important to acknowledge and address those realities. But there are at least as many times when these two areas work synergistically—times when teaching for creativity is one of the *best* ways to promote skill development and knowledge acquisition. We ignore such opportunities and synergies at our (and our students') peril.

The potential conflict between creativity and content is part of long-standing disputes about the relationship between learning content and learning to think more effectively. It is also related to enduring questions about the possibilities of transfer of learning, and teaching to promote such transfer. We won't pretend that those disputes have been settled, but in recent years it has become more clear that thinking depends quite heavily on knowledge; that mistakes in everyday critical thinking are more often the result of faulty premises (i.e., incorrect factual knowledge) than a lack of general problem-solving skills; and that teaching for transfer requires a great deal of context-specific training or practice in any domain to which transfer is desired.

Content knowledge is essential to thinking—one cannot think in a content-free vacuum—so teaching content-free thinking skills is impossible. This is as true in teaching creativity as it is in teaching any other thinking skill. To teach a creative cognitive skill like divergent thinking requires focusing on *something* in particular (content). Higher-level thinking often requires automatization of lower-level skills. To improve students' thinking (including creative thinking) in a given domain, teachers must provide factual content about that domain as well as develop domain-specific cognitive skills.

So we must teach students content knowledge if we want to improve their thinking. Conversely, the best way to teach content knowledge is to get students to *think about the subject* in some way—to become actively engaged with the content. But this consistent finding of cognitive and educational psychologists doesn't quite tell us *how* to teach; after all, we hope that no one is really arguing in favor of the mindless rote memorization of unconnected facts. Today, most educators are constructivists, at least in the most basic sense. That is to say that learning requires a student to construct or create meaning based on experiences in his or her own mind. Being actively engaged with the content to be learned means active *cognitive* engagement. However, the need for active cognitive engagement does not address such diverse methods as reciprocal teaching, discovery learning, sitting quietly reading a book, cooperative learning, and even listening to a lecture (which, if one is actually listening, requires attending to and interpreting the material in terms of what one already knows and leads to assimilation of knowledge and accommodation of new cognitive structures). Research shows that learning requires active cognitive engagement and that meaningful learning is more effective than mindless memorization of uncomprehended facts. Thus, an emphasis on content knowledge does not conflict with an emphasis on active processing of information; in fact, one requires the other.

Thus, the Common Core State Standards are *not* bad news for those who wish to emphasize the development of thinking skills, despite the proposed rivalry between the two. But what about creativity? The Common Core requires learning a basic set of knowledge and facts as well as developing specific content-based skills. But this requirement does not interfere with the development of creative thinking. Teachers who too readily accept the notion that teaching the Common Core means they must jettison creativity will be sacrificing their students' development as creative thinkers. Further, they will also make it more difficult for students to acquire the skills and knowledge outlined in the Common Core State Standards because these teachers are giving up some of the most powerful tools available for helping students acquire such knowledge and skills.

The implication of focusing on content knowledge and skills is the same for creativity as it is for other kinds of thinking. Having richer and more extensive content knowledge and skills should support, not detract from, creative thinking, just as such knowledge and skills support other kinds of thinking. Creativity researchers and theorists agree that creative achievement—especially creative genius—requires extensive content knowledge. As psychology's prolific expert on creative genius, Dean Keith Simonton (1994), wrote: "There are no shortcuts to greatness. A person who aims to achieve anything of worth must learn, study, and practice" (p. 68).

Domain-specific knowledge and skills are also crucial for the more garden-variety creativity that all of us share to varying degrees. Many of our creative-thinking abilities are fairly narrow in their application. For example, even the cognitive skills underlying creative performance in writing short stories and in writing nonfiction appear to be surprisingly different (e.g., Kaufman, 2002).

So creativity requires skills and knowledge (as promoted by the Common Core State Standards). But how does teaching for creativity promote the acquisition of such (Common Core–like) knowledge and skills?

Let's look at a very practical application of the more abstract idea that teaching for creativity can promote acquisition of Common Core skills. Consider the most widely taught creative thinking skill: divergent thinking. What better way to help students build their Phonological Awareness—which is one of the four basic strands of the kindergarten Common Core State Standards (CCSS.ELA-Literacy.RF.K.2. Demonstrate understanding of spoken words, syllables, and sounds [phonemes]. National Governors Association Center for Best Practices [NGACBP] & Council of Chief State School

Officers [CCSSO], 2014b)—than by having students brainstorm words that begin with particular phonemes?

"Let's think of all the words we can that begin with the same sound as *fire* and *friend*" is a divergent-thinking exercise, but it's also a phoneme-learning activity par excellence. Or else think about the task of finding different ways to express equalities (as in CCSS.Math.Content.HSA-CED.A.4. Rearrange formulas to highlight a quantity of interest, using the same reasoning as in solving equations [NGACBP & CCSSO, 2014c]). Doesn't this seem like both a prime example of creative thinking that requires content knowledge and also what Bloom (1956) would have termed "application and synthesis," key components of creative thinking?

Creativity requires the skills and knowledge that the Common Core State Standards were designed to promote, and teachers can and should use creative-thinking activities as ways to help their students learn the skills and knowledge of the Common Core. A marriage made in heaven? Well, not exactly—as we said, there are times when teaching for creativity and teaching for the Common Core will conflict (and we will explore ways to deal with these conflicts)—but most of the time they fit together like the foreground and the background of a landscape painting. Which is foreground and which is background? It depends on the particular situation, but the basic answer is both: Creativity can provide the background to help students gain knowledge and skills of the CCSSI, and this CCSSI background provides many of the tools students need to apply their creative thinking.

In the chapters that follow, we discuss common conceptions and challenges facing teachers interested in promoting creativity (Chapter 1), discuss relevant theories and research on creativity in the classroom (Chapters 2 and 3), and highlight ways to maintain creativity while following the CCSS (Chapters 4–7). More specifically, in Chapter 1 we discuss how popular conceptions often place creativity and standards on opposite ends of a false dichotomy where one can only exist at the expense of the other. In Chapter 2, we then discuss how this problematic conception is out of step with the empirical research about creativity. Indeed, scholars generally agree that creativity can be defined as something that is both new and appropriate to the task as determined in a particular sociocultural context (Plucker, Beghetto, & Dow, 2004; Sternberg, Kaufman, & Pretz, 2002). In other words, basic novelty is not enough. Moreover, creative achievement is domain specific, requires deep knowledge of subject matter, and involves constraints (Baer & Garrett, 2010; Sternberg & Kaufman, 2010).

In Chapter 3, we discuss how teaching for creativity and the Common Core requires establishing a supportive learning environment. This includes discussing and providing examples of how teachers can avoid "killing" creativity. Specifically, we draw on the creativity-motivation research (Amabile,

1996; Hennessey, 2010a, 2010b) to provide examples and recommendations for developing CCSSI-based lessons and learning activities that support (rather than inadvertently suppress) creative expression.

In Chapters 4 and 5, we explore how Common Core English Language Arts (ELA) and Mathematics standards enable students to develop their subject matter understanding while at the same time develop their creative potential. Vignettes will show how some teachers have successfully incorporated creativity into teaching the ELA and Mathematics standards. We also offer suggestions, tips, and actual lesson plans for elementary, middle, and secondary teachers endeavoring to teach standards-based lessons more creatively. We also discuss how to modify existing classroom assessments to serve these dual purposes.

In Chapter 6, we offer additional information for incorporating creativity into teaching, including more detailed discussion of types of instructional activities that teachers can use (e.g., design projects and simulations), explanations of ways that various academic subject areas can be combined with Common Core State Standards, and ideas for assessing creativity and Common Core learning. Moreover, we discuss teaching for creativity in diverse populations and provide a synthesis of tips and ideas presented throughout the book. This summary serves as a quick reference. The chapter closes with a brief annotated bibliography of resources about creativity and its role in the classroom.

Our goal in writing this book is not to try to convince readers that either the Common Core State Standards or creativity is fundamentally good or bad. Both have costs and benefits, and we endeavor to provide a balanced presentation of each. Our aim is to help educators understand how they might better support student creativity in the context of content standards in general and the Common Core State Standards in particular.

CHAPTER 1

Creativity and the Common Core
Hidden Beliefs and Common Misconceptions

**Vignette 1: Should Teachers Establish a
Separate "Creativity Time" in Their Curriculum?**

Mr. Marrow is a 1st-grade teacher who values creativity and often incorporates it into his teaching. Although he readily admits that he doesn't know much about creativity theory or research, he has worked hard over the years to make room for creative expression in his classroom. In fact, he long ago established "creativity time" wherein students can do any kind of art project or other form of self-expression. He teaches his students when to be silly and when to get serious. As such, he often gives his students cues to remind them when they are being "creative" but "not appropriate" given the academic goals of a particular lesson. Mr. Marrow has noticed that he has to give these types of cues more often since his school adopted the Common Core. He feels that his creativity/academic content ratio is a bit out of balance—particularly when teaching reading and mathematics. He is trying to find more time for his students to take small breaks from the content so that they can still find ways to express themselves creatively. Unfortunately, he feels it is a losing battle. He is starting to feel torn in two different directions.

**Vignette 2: Is Creativity Really Compatible with
Standards-Based Teaching?**

Ms. Pascal, a high school math teacher, often mentions to her colleagues that she inevitably gets one or two "creative" students in each section of the courses she teaches. For her, creative students are those who continually pose interesting questions and frequently surprise her with the depth of their mathematical insights. She feels that creative students' strengths are also what make them so challenging to teach. They are at times exhausting, interesting, engaged, disruptive, and simply difficult to predict. The thought of increasing her students' creative behavior is one that sounds good in theory, but not when facing six sections of students and trying to keep on pace with all the new Common Core Mathematics standards. Ms. Pascal is convinced that teaching for creativity means not teaching the Common Core State Standards. She feels both are reasonable, but incompatible, goals: Whereas creativity is unconstrained originality, the Common Core is constrained conformity.

Mr. Marrow's and Ms. Pascal's experiences illustrate how many teachers feel: caught between competing curricular goals in light of the new Common Core State Standards. This chapter will take a closer look at common beliefs about creativity and content standards, specifically the Common Core. We will discuss how some of these beliefs can result in mistakenly viewing creativity and standards-based learning as competing priorities. We will also discuss how a greater understanding of creativity can increase a teacher's ability to incorporate creativity development into standards-based teaching. The chapter will close with a *From Concepts to Classroom* section, which will summarize practical tips and suggestions for how teachers might incorporate these insights and ideas into their classrooms.

COMMON BELIEFS ABOUT CREATIVITY

Creativity is a tricky concept to understand, particularly in the context of the classroom. One reason is that teachers, like most people, hold their own beliefs about creativity. Sometimes these beliefs are in alignment with how creativity researchers define and understand creativity; at other times they conflict. These personal, often unspoken thoughts that people have about a topic are called implicit beliefs. Implicit beliefs can be positive or negative. Psychological research has found that people's expressed opinions often correspond with their implicit beliefs about controversial issues (such as racism or politics) (Greenwald & Banaji, 1995).

People have implicit beliefs about creativity as well. One landmark study by Sternberg (1985) found that people generally view creativity as distinct from intelligence. They associated creativity with four dimensions: nonentrenchment (i.e., willingness to do something differently), aesthetic taste/imagination, perspicacity (astuteness), and inquisitiveness. Some studies have shown that some of the explicit theories of creativity, which will be discussed in detail in the next chapter, are intuitively believed by laypeople (e.g., Kaufman & Beghetto, 2013a).

There have been few formal studies of people's implicit beliefs about the content standards—but this does not mean that people do not have strong opinions!

COMMON BELIEFS ABOUT CONTENT STANDARDS

The Common Core State Standards are the latest iteration of the standards-based movement in the United States, which began with the Elementary and Secondary Education Act of 1965 (Shepard, 2009), though the Common Core State Standards are not the result of federal legislation. Rather, the Common Core was (and continues to be) led by the National Governors Association and the Council of Chief State School Officers, with input from teachers, parents, school administrators, and various experts from across the country (NGACPB & CCSSO, 2014a). The Common Core aims to better prepare all students for entrance into postsecondary education and the workforce by outlining a common roadmap of concepts that students need to learn regardless of their geographic location.

Despite the fact that the Common Core stems from educators rather than legislators, the public views it with suspicion. Politicians have used the Common Core as an opportunity to establish partisan points of contention (Bidwell, 2014). Further, educators—even supporters of the approach—have raised questions about content coverage (Porter, McMaken, Hwang, & Yang, 2011), implementation, and assessment (American Federation of Teachers, 2013; Strauss, 2013).

These concerns aside, adoption of the Common Core State Standards has moved forward and many teachers have been busy incorporating them into their everyday curricula. While many policymakers and commentators may continue to debate the merits of the Common Core from their armchairs, many more teachers are being asked to bring them to life. We direct this book to teachers who are working with the Common Core and want to maintain both creativity and meaningful learning. To explore this, we must start with an understanding of creativity and content standards.

As discussed, many people view creativity as unconstrained originality. We say, for instance, "Think outside of the box." Creativity is often associated with freedom, expansiveness, and divergence. Content standards, on the other hand, are often seen as curricular constraints—or the very "box" that creative students (and teachers) try to escape. They are sometimes viewed as narrow, limiting, and restrictive. As a result, teachers feel stuck in the middle between a desire to teach for creativity and a professional responsibility to teach for the attainment of content standards.

One of the authors of this book (Beghetto) recently held a workshop with teachers who were interested in teaching for creativity. During the lunch break a teacher (whom we will call Ms. Ortiz) shared a story about her experiences teaching in a school with a nearly singular focus on meeting content standards. Ms. Ortiz is passionately committed to teaching for and with creativity, but felt she had little freedom to do so. In fact, she explained that the only time teachers can work without surveillance and disruption from school administrators is when they display a "practice testing in progress" sign on their classroom door.

Practice testing in Ms. Ortiz's school is viewed as a sacred time. Taking advantage of the way the administration takes a "hands-off" approach when they believe students are doing practice exams, Ms. Ortiz used this time to engage her students in creative curricular activities. Ms. Ortiz and other teachers who are passionate about creativity will do whatever it takes to incorporate it into the curriculum.

By contrast, Gary Groth, a veteran teacher with more than 30 years of experience, described his most recent year of teaching as the "absolute worst year in the classroom" he had ever experienced. Not because of his students, but because of how he experienced external curricular mandates: "This year I was told what to teach, when to teach, how to teach, how long to teach, who to teach, who not to teach, and how often to test. My students were assessed with easily more than 120 tests of one shape or another within the first six months of the school year" (Groth, cited in Berliner, 2011, p. 85).

Ms. Ortiz and Mr. Groth found that content standards can serve as a vehicle for developing policies that place unnecessary pressure on teachers (and their students). Moreover, the concomitant evaluation, monitoring, and comparison that sometimes accompany accountability mandates often kill the motivation necessary for creative expression (Amabile, 1996; Hennessey, 2010a, 2010b). As a result, some teachers sneak creativity into their classrooms on the sly, whereas others may simply become discouraged.

These external pressures can also result in a narrowing of the curriculum (Berliner, 2011) which, in turn, undermines meaningful learning. Rather than teaching students how to learn and how to think, the curriculum becomes focused on a narrow range of outcomes. For example, McNeil (2000) found that teachers' most immediate responses to external curricular mandates was to narrow the scope and quality of course content—thereby distancing students from more meaningful and active learning. This narrow focus is most profoundly felt, according to McNeil, by students in low-income and predominately ethnic and racial minority neighborhoods. In this way, the Common Core exacerbates long-standing inequalities in education.

We recognize that implementing standards-based reforms can increase pressures on teachers and students and narrow the curriculum. As such, those leaders and policymakers who would advocate for creativity need to support teachers' efforts by examining how teachers experience such external mandates and exploring ways to decrease external pressures. We also feel it is important not to deny the agency that most teachers have in their own classrooms. Indeed, teachers can still do much to support student creativity and meaningful learning in the context of the Common Core. We will present ideas and examples for how this might be accomplished throughout the remainder of this book. Prior to doing so, however, it is important that we first return to the question of whether creativity and the Common Core are compatible.

CONTENT STANDARDS AND CREATIVITY: IRRECONCILABLE DIFFERENCES?

Are creativity and the Common Core State Standards incompatible? We think not—in fact, we will argue that there are many synergies, places where the Standards and creativity support, reinforce, and enhance one another. One needn't abandon creativity, one needn't forego many opportunities to teach students to be more imaginative, and one needn't feel like a philistine by teaching to the Common Core. But a teacher does need to be a bit more thoughtful about how he or she teaches for creativity, a bit more selective about the kinds of exercises and activities used, and a bit more creative in the ways in which he or she plans lessons. All in a day's work for a teacher.

We are not Pollyannas; therefore, we are not arguing that we are living in the best of all possible (educational) worlds. And we acknowledge that there will be times when teaching for creativity and teaching to the Common Core will conflict. For example, to encourage students' creativity we often want to avoid extrinsic constraints (like rewards and evaluation) as much as possible, whereas the development of skills (including many of the Common Core skills) often requires frequent and thoughtful evaluation of students' work. But that conflict existed long before the Common Core came along, and even the most passionate advocates of creativity enhancement acknowledge that students need to develop skills and acquire knowledge—domain-specific material that (among other things) is necessary for improving creative performance. Even Shakespeare had to learn history (and how to write and spell) somewhere along the way before he could write *Henry IV*. Denying our students opportunities to learn such things wouldn't just cause them to fail Common Core–based tests. It would also limit their creative growth. We will discuss ways to deal with this intrinsic versus extrinsic motivation issue and other potential creativity/Common Core conflicts below. They are manageable, but dealing with such conflicts productively requires thoughtful planning.

So yes, there are some conflicts between teaching for creativity and teaching the Common Core, but they are fewer than most teachers imagine. Many of the seeming conflicts between the Common Core and creativity are based on misunderstandings. There are four kinds of misunderstandings that lead people to think that content standards such as the Common Core State Standards and creativity are incompatible. These misunderstandings can make teachers feel that they can either promote the skills and content knowledge outlined in the Common Core State Standards *or* promote creativity, but not both. Here we present those four misconceptions, stated in somewhat extreme versions to help make them clear:

1. Creativity means that there are no wrong answers, and teaching for creativity means valuing only the wildest and most unusual ideas.
2. The Common Core State Standards are lists of things students need to know, and learning them will require lots of rote memorization.
3. The best way to acquire knowledge and skills is via drill-and-kill.
4. The best way to promote creativity is to be silly.

Okay, those are caricatures—we said we would state them in extreme versions—but the beliefs of many teachers are often just tamer versions of these misconceptions. Let's examine them one at a time.

1. Creativity means that there are no wrong answers, and teaching for creativity means valuing only the wildest and most unusual ideas. It is true that creative thinking often involves coming up with many possible responses to open-ended questions—that creativity often requires (among other things) divergent thinking. Divergent thinking is often conflated with brainstorming, but brainstorming is actually a technique—one of many techniques— designed to elicit divergent thinking. It is particularly common to use this technique when trying to get a group to engage in divergent thinking. And it is also true that during brainstorming, participants are encouraged to defer or suspend judgment and accept equally (for the time being) every idea that comes to mind. But divergent thinking (whether produced by brainstorming or some other method) is just one part of the creative process. Some creativity-training programs have stressed divergent thinking and de-emphasized convergent and evaluative thinking. But this is not a problem with creativity; it's a problem with having a very limited understanding of the creative process. Successful creativity involves multiple iterations of both divergent and convergent thinking. For example, students may first engage in brainstorming or divergent thinking at the problem construction stage—simply figuring out what the problem is that needs to be solved (e.g., Reiter-Palmon & Robinson, 2009). Convergent thinking can help choose the best problem to tackle; divergent thinking can then be used again to figure out ways that the problem might be solved. Convergent thinking can select a best pathway—and so on, with multiple iterations leading to the best possible creative solution.

Ask almost any creativity researcher these days to define creativity and they'll tell you that creativity involves coming up with new ideas *that work* (or words to that effect). We put *"that work"* in italics to emphasize an important point: Creativity isn't the same as finding *the* right answer, but it is very much about finding (or inventing) right (good, appropriate, successful, workable, desirable, suitable) answers—answers that work, that get the job done, that fit the constraints of the situations, that solve the problem. Producing many wild and unusual ideas may or may not be part of that process. But creativity isn't about ignoring the real world and coming up with ideas that are unworkable, and it often requires a great deal of knowledge and skill—the kinds of things the Common Core State Standards are all about.

It is also important to note that a new idea does not mean a perfectly unique idea. If a child figures out a different way to tie her shoes, that's an innovation as long as she figured it out herself, even if other people figured it out long ago. It's innovation if it's new to her—and if it *works* in some way. If it doesn't work—if it leaves her shoelaces in a messy, tangled, and ugly knot—then her efforts may qualify as imaginative, or even as a good try, and she may learn through the process things she will need to know to move on to a better solution, but what she has done is not creative in the sense we mean here. The work done by a creative idea may be very small— it may be simply thinking about a problem in a slightly different way that allows new perspectives or insights; it may mean constructing meaning out of something that was previously not understood or misunderstood; it may be realizing something that was apparent to others but not to oneself—but it must do *something*. Creativity doesn't mean that every idea is equal to every other idea, even if one suspends judgment for a period of time while generating possible solutions and even if in the service of producing a few creative ideas one decides to treat every idea, temporarily, as a good idea. Suspending or deferring judgment just means the evaluation will come later. The misconception of considering divergent thinking to be the entirety of creativity minimizes the importance of skills, knowledge, and the need for ideas that actually work in the production of creative things.

2. The Common Core State Standards are lists of things students need to know, and learning them will require lots of rote memorization. There may be some standards in the Common Core that look like lists, but for the most part that is not what the Common Core State Standards are about at all, and memorization is not the primary skill one needs to meet the Standards in the Common Core. The Common Core is really about skills and understandings, which are not abilities that one can normally acquire via memorization. The Standards require students to be able to do things with knowledge, to know when it's appropriate do one thing versus another, to be able to think original thoughts in a domain in ways that work. Here are three skills (the first three) in the grade 3 English language arts standards for reading literature:

> ➤ CCSS.ELA-Literacy.RL.3.1. Ask and answer questions to demonstrate understanding of a text, referring explicitly to the text as the basis for the answers.
> ➤ CCSS.ELA-Literacy.RL.3.2. Recount stories, including fables, folktales, and myths from diverse cultures; determine the central message, lesson, or moral and explain how it is conveyed through key details in the text.
> ➤ CCSS.ELA-Literacy.RL.3.3. Describe characters in a story (e.g., their traits, motivations, or feelings) and explain how their actions contribute to the sequence of events. (NGACPB & CCSSO, 2014b)

None of these are things one could accomplish by memorizing anything; all require figuring something out, coming up with ideas—ideas that work, that are based on the text in question—that have *not* been stated explicitly. This requires understanding, but it requires more than just understanding. Students must be able to do things *with* that understanding. They need to do things independently. They need to do things that allow them to come up with answers they have not been given. Doesn't that sound a lot like creative thinking? And this isn't just in the English Language Arts Standards. Here's one from the Grade 8 Math Standards:

> ➤ CCSS.Math.Content.8.F.B.4. Construct a function to model a linear relationship between two quantities. Determine the rate of change and initial value of the function from a description of a relationship or from two (x, y) values, including reading these from a table or from a graph. Interpret the rate of change and initial value of a linear function in terms of the situation it models, and in terms of its graph or a table of values. (NGACPB & CCSSO, 2014c)

Constructing a function to model a linear relationship between two quantities requires very interesting, challenging, and resourceful thinking—not memorization—and it's not something students can learn by rote memorization. It requires understanding a number of things, figuring out how to use them, and coming up with answers students have not been given, answers that fit the specific situation described in the problem. Isn't that a lot like the seven words we said were a key to creativity: "coming up with new ideas that work"?

3. The best way to acquire knowledge and skills is via drill-and-kill. Okay, nobody really thinks that—at least no one will confess to thinking that—and yet people who care intensely about creativity often go overboard in their critiques of teaching methods that do require memorization. For example, in the CCSS students need to do these things:

➤ CCSS.Math.Content.K.CC.A.1. Count to 100 by ones and by tens.
➤ CCSS.Math.Content.K.CC.A.2. Count forward beginning from a given number within the known sequence (instead of having to begin at 1).
➤ CCSS.Math.Content.K.CC.A.3. Write numbers from 0 to 20. Represent a number of objects with a written numeral 0–20 (with 0 representing a count of no objects). (NGACPB & CCSSO, 2014c)

Memorization and drills are likely to be involved in learning this material. But most of the knowledge and skills in the CCSS are not things one could successfully teach via drills and repetition. Most skills and knowledge are not acquired most easily or most successfully via drills and repetition. Most skills and knowledge are acquired by using and applying them in a variety of situations, thinking about them in ways that connect them to what one already knows, recalling them in appropriate situations, and analyzing them to understand them better. In sum, most skills and knowledge are acquired by thinking (including creative thinking), not by rote memorization. The Common Core State Standards are not about rote memorization, and drill-and-kill should play little part in teaching to those Standards.

4. The best way to promote creativity is to be silly. It's true that some divergent thinking activities can lead to silliness, and a bit of silliness is sometimes okay, but the goal of divergent thinking (which, bear in mind, is just one part of creative thinking) is to come up with many varied responses to an open-ended prompt or question. If divergent thinking is being used in the service of solving a real problem, then one would hope and assume that the ideas generated would be usable. As a warm-up activity when teaching students a divergent thinking method such as brainstorming, a teacher might ask students to do things like think of unusual uses for a brick (this is probably the most common exemplar of a brainstorming activity, unfortunately; as a warm-up activity it's fine, but it does lend itself to silliness). But brainstorming (and other methods of encouraging divergent thinking) can be serious, silly, and everything in between, depending on the situation. In classrooms, divergent thinking can be a powerful tool to help students figure things out. For example, consider this standard:

> ➤ CCSS.ELA-Literacy.RST.11-12.5. Analyze how the text structures information or ideas into categories or hierarchies, demonstrating understanding of the information or ideas. (NGACPB & CCSSO, 2014b)

One might start by answering this question: "What are the important ideas in this passage?" After listing as many as one can (divergent thinking) and deciding which are the most important ones on the list (evaluative thinking), one might then ask oneself this question: "What are some different categories one might use to sort these ideas?" After listing several possibilities (divergent thinking) one might then decide which set of categories will work best for this text (evaluative thinking) and then use those to sort the ideas from the first list into the categories. The kinds of divergent thinking one might use in making this type of analysis are not at all silly, but this is still very much divergent thinking—and to do this analysis well will require a great deal of creative thinking that involves both divergent and evaluative processes.

So, are we saying that we needn't worry, that creativity and the Common Core are natural partners? Not exactly. It is important to see that creativity and CCSS can be allies. We must recognize that they are not natural enemies (as too many people are wont to assume). Next, we need to look for all the synergies we can find. The steps that a teacher would take to promote creativity are not always the same as what she or he does to develop the kinds of skills and knowledge outlined in the Common Core; sometimes they may even conflict. But the important thing is to find ways in which creativity and the goals of the CCSS *can* work together. There are ways that teaching for one will promote the other. One of our major goals for this book is to help teachers teach for both.

CONCLUDING THOUGHTS

The goal of combining creativity and the Common Core is attainable. However, in order to do so we need to be able to understand and overcome several conceptual barriers. The purpose of this chapter was to uncover several hidden beliefs that can impede teachers' best efforts at simultaneously addressing Common Core State Standards and supporting creativity in their classrooms. When teachers are aware of these beliefs and misconceptions they are in a better position to overcome them so that they can attain the goal of teaching the Common Core more creatively. Doing so also involves developing a deeper understanding of creativity and its role in the classroom, which is the focus of the next chapter.

FROM CONCEPTS TO CLASSROOM

We've covered much ground in this chapter. In this section, we summarize a few of the key concepts discussed and provide some reminders for how these concepts can be applied to the classroom.

- *Creativity can thrive within constraints.* Creativity is often viewed as synonymous with unconstrained originality. When this happens it is difficult for teachers, like those in the opening vignettes, to imagine how creativity might have a role in the teaching of academic subject matter. As will be discussed in Chapter 2, creativity can be thought of as originality expressed within the conventions and constraints of academic subject matter. During math class, for example, teachers can ask students to come up with as many ways as they can to solve a particular problem. The multiple solutions represent the expression of originality; requiring that the solutions also be mathematically accurate would represent the academic constraints.
- *The Common Core is more than rote memorization.* The skills needed to succeed at the Common Core State Standards require deep learning, critical thinking, and understanding. When analyzing the actual descriptions from the CCSSI, it is clear that creativity would usually be an asset, not a hindrance.
- *Everyone has creative potential.* Some people (such as the teacher in Vignette 2) may believe that only certain students are creative. Creativity is a human trait shared by all people. Nurturing creativity in the classroom starts with recognizing that not only do all of our students have creative potential, but we, as teachers, also have creative potential. This can help us understand that creative students are not necessarily disruptive students, although they sometimes can be. As we will discuss in Chapter 2, sometimes students will benefit from being encouraged to be more creative (e.g., "Okay, now come up with your own story"), and at other times students will benefit from understanding when their efforts at creative expression do not fit the context (e.g., "Your poem about the beauty of prime numbers is compelling, but writing it instead of an equation on your algebra exam is not the appropriate venue for sharing it").
- *Teachers can attain Common Core State Standards in multiple ways.* Educators sometimes associate standards-based teaching with rote memorization. One reason is because this is typically how students' proficiency with standards has been assessed on external tests. Although memorization of facts has its place in learning, it

need not be the only thing we focus on when teaching. Just as there are multiple roads to Rome, there are many ways to teach the Common Core State Standards. Standards do not prescribe how teachers should teach, but rather provide guidance on the content that should be taught. We recognize that in some school districts, teachers can also feel pressure in how they teach. In most cases, however, teachers still have the professional agency to decide how to teach. They should have the freedom to choose to teach in ways that have a basis in research or, at the very least, a sound instructional rationale. In Chapter 6, we discuss a few key instructional principles and techniques that we view as particularly promising for simultaneously teaching creativity and standards-based learning. Regardless of the technique, however, it is typically a good idea when trying out new approaches to let students, parents, colleagues, and administrators know the instructional approaches being used and the rationale for them.

- *Creative thinking involves serious academic work.* Being creative can be fun. But it isn't *just* fun. Being creative requires follow-through, hard work, effort, and mastering domain-appropriate content. Advice to aspiring creative writers, for example, nearly always says that one must read, write, rewrite, and then repeat. It is (comparatively) easy to get a good idea. It is much harder to figure out which idea merits your time and to devote yourself to developing and executing a plan.

- *Creativity is compatible with standards-based learning.* When we broaden our understanding of creativity and content standards we can recognize how they are compatible (rather than competing) educational goals. Throughout the remainder of this book we will continue to discuss and attempt to demonstrate this connection, but we also stress that recognizing that the connection is possible is an important first step. By simply starting with the question "what if?" it is possible to generate new possibilities and surprise oneself with the various ways that creativity can be incorporated into Common Core lessons. Oftentimes even the smallest of changes to existing lessons can result in opportunities for creative expression. In English Language Arts (ELA), for instance, in addition to having students demonstrate their comprehension by paraphrasing what happened in a particular story, you can also ask them to explain what would happen if they changed one event or removed a particular character. This not only challenges them to engage more deeply with the existing narrative, but also provides an opportunity for creative thinking.

CHAPTER 2

Understanding Creativity in the Classroom

Getting Beyond Hidden Beliefs and Misconceptions

Vignette 1: Must We Limit Originality with Cold Facts?

Mr. Luce and Ms. Phakt are discussing how to deal with factual errors in the history essays their students have recently written. Mr. Luce says that the factual details aren't really that important to him, and if students can make an interesting and original argument, he doesn't worry too much that some of their supporting evidence may be historically incorrect. "I don't want to kill their creativity," he argues. Ms. Phakt agrees that an interesting, original, and well-argued essay is a wonderful thing, but she worries that not correcting students' historical errors could lead to problems for them down the road.

Vignette 2: Is It Ever Okay to Stifle Creativity?

Sammy is constantly interrupting Ms. Kayas's class with unusual questions about the things the class is learning in science. For example, when they were studying the solar system Sammy wanted to know how each of the planets got its name; when they were learning about constellations he wanted to know if these same constellation names were used in non-Western countries. Ms. Kayas tries to answer all of Sammy's questions, but she often doesn't know the answers, and even when she does it often takes a good deal of class time to explain those answers. The questions are often unusual ones and Ms. Kayas values Sammy's originality and curiosity, but sometimes it seems that the whole point of the questions is to get her off track (which she admits often happens). Ms. Kayas's colleague Mr. Sato suggests that rather than answer Sammy's questions, she give Sammy the assignment of researching each question of this type that he asks and then reporting his answers to the class. Ms. Kayas fears that this will seem like a punishment and may stifle Sammy's imagination and inquisitive spirit, both of which she wants to encourage.

Creativity has traditionally been defined as having two key components (e.g., Barron, 1955; Guilford, 1950). The first is originality—how new or different is something? Repetition is not creative. Most people intuitively grasp this part; even if Einstein (allegedly) said that creativity is hiding your sources, a plagiarized idea would be unlikely to be held up as creative. The second aspect of creativity is being task appropriate. A block of wood is not a creative dinner, nor is spaghetti a creative building component. They are both certainly original, but neither fulfills the basic requirement needed for the task at hand. It is important to note that task appropriateness does not mean socially appropriate. Macaroni with chocolate may not be standard fare, but it is edible; a house painted a shocking fuchsia color is no more likely to collapse than a more traditional one.

Both of these concepts are needed for something to be considered creative. Simonton (2013) presents it as an equation: Creativity = Originality × Appropriateness. If either originality or appropriateness is zero (like a plagiarized paper or serving a brick for dinner), then it can't be creative. Based on the works of Beghetto & Kaufman (2014) and Plucker, Beghetto, and Dow (2004), we would slightly elaborate on this equation to include context: $C = [O \times A]_{context}$. Whether or not something should be considered original or task appropriate (and, therefore, creative) is determined by the particular social, cultural, and historical context in which it is produced.

CREATIVITY: A BRIEF THEORETICAL OVERVIEW

There are many other ways of conceptualizing the construct of creativity. Rhodes (1962) proposed the Four P's—person, process, product, and press (e.g., the surrounding environment, such as the classroom) as a framework. This basic paradigm—addressing who is creative, how we can be creative, what is creative, and how creativity can be nurtured (or stifled)—is a handy way of sorting through what can be a vast and occasionally disjointed research literature.

Glaveanu (2013) recently extended the Four P's into the Five A's (actor, action, artifact, audience, and affordances), with an emphasis on how social and cultural context plays a role in creativity. Three of the Four P's map relatively directly. The person becomes the actor, the process becomes the action, and the product becomes the artifact. The press is split into two concepts:

audience and affordances. The audience refers to the people who respond to the creative work (from immediate peers to a global network of millions) and affordances are the specific materials (or lack thereof) that a person can access.

Another approach to thinking about creativity is to think about whose creativity is being studied—although a 1st-grade student and Mozart both fall under "person" in the Four-P approach, they are obviously quite different. Creativity research has traditionally distinguished between two levels: everyday (or "little-c") creativity and genius-level (or "Big-C") creativity. Kaufman and Beghetto (2009, 2013a; Beghetto & Kaufman, 2007, 2013) have built off this dichotomy to propose a fuller approach with the Four-C Model of Creativity (mini-c, little-c, Pro-c, and Big-C).

Mini-c: Personal Creativity

The first level, mini-c or personal creativity, represents the personal insights that are part of the learning process. These subjective self-discoveries are meaningful to the person, even if other people may not recognize the ideas as being creative. A child might experience mini-c when writing a haiku or proposing an algebraic proof for the first time, yet mini-c is not restricted to children. Adults may go on the same personal journeys—indeed, a teacher may feel mini-c when teaching a new lesson.

Something can be mini-c even if it does not meet the traditionally defined markers of "new" and "appropriate" (as long as it is personally new and appropriate). Vygotsky (1967/2004) argued that internal creative acts can still be creative, even if they only embody "some mental or emotional construct that lives within the person who created it and is known only to him" (p. 7).

We will take a little extra time with mini-c as it is the level of creativity most relevant to schools, yet also easy to overlook. One of the best ways of fostering creative potential is to recognize and appreciate mini-c ideas. Teachers who effectively teach for creativity recognize and invite students' mini-c insights, interpretations, and ideas whenever they are introducing a new concept or starting a new lesson.

A group of creativity researches in Korea (Cho et al., 2013), for example, documented how teachers encouraged mini-c creativity by inviting students to draw on their own experiences to understand and interpret newly introduced academic concepts and to think about subjects from multiple perspectives. One such teacher, for instance, explained, "To nurture student creativity I pay more attention [to] posing questions so that they can think about the subject from many different angles . . . I prefer to teach in a way that allows the students to talk about what they think or feel because even their trivial thoughts have their own reasons" (p. 159).

Another teacher explained, "I try to give students tasks in which they can challenge themselves and approach from different angles so that they can think in different ways" (p. 161). This teacher also delayed calling on students who usually provided more standardized or expected answers so that other students wouldn't immediately converge on a single, standard answer (Cho et al., 2013). Doing so provided the time and curricular space for students to develop and express their own unique and personally meaningful interpretations, ideas, and insights.

The key to teaching in ways that are supportive of mini-c creativity is to infuse opportunities for mini-c expression in the context of everyday, academic-subject matter. This is perhaps most clearly illustrated in how a Grade 5 Science teacher in Cho et al.'s (2013) study approached science. The teacher would invite students to creatively reinterpret new information or situations based on concepts they had learned—expecting her students simultaneously to express their mini-c ideas and "think and express thoughts logically and with reason" (p. 162).

When teachers invite students to share their unique interpretations and insights they are establishing a safe environment for their students. This, in turn, increases the willingness with which students will take the risks necessary for learning and creative expression (Beghetto, 2009). These risks can extend from simply speaking up in class to arguing potentially unpopular stances. Once students feel comfortable sharing their mini-c ideas, teachers can then help students take the next step by developing those mini-c insights into little-c contributions. Are their ideas feasible? Are they plans that students can develop with their current resources, or are they dreams to be visited and revisited on the road to adulthood? Are they flights of fancy or watershed moments that may help shape a life's path?

Vignette 1 exemplifies the tension teachers sometimes feel when inviting students to think creatively about a topic. Students' ideas may sometimes be interesting, but may also be based on factually incorrect premises. There is no single right way to deal with such situations. We encourage teachers to sometimes do what Mr. Luce suggests—not worry too much at first about confused facts when students offer an interesting idea—but also to make sure that at some point students do get their facts straight. The situation is in some ways comparable to how teachers use invented spelling, a technique employed by many early childhood teachers to encourage very young students to be writers by telling them to spell words as best they can but not worry too much if they are correctly spelled or not. Allowing errors can be freeing, and the goal is to get students to start writing and to see themselves as writers. But even with invented spelling, later in the composition process students will need to clean up their work. In the case of creative ideas based in part on factual errors, teachers can commend and discuss an interesting idea based on incorrect facts and later show the student that the theory or idea will need more work by explaining the actual facts that are relevant to the theory or idea.

Helping students develop their mini-c ideas requires taking a few extra moments to hear what students are saying. Vivian Paley has described how she eventually came to recognize the importance of carefully listening to her students. Moreover, she quickly recognized that student creativity presented itself in every lesson: "The rules of teaching had changed; I now wanted to hear the answers I could not myself invent . . . Indeed, the inventions tumbled out as if they simply had been waiting for me to stop talking and begin listening" (Paley, 2007, p. 155).

Listening to students will not guarantee the discovery of creative insights. Sometimes teachers may need to provide further encouragement for students to provide their own unique perspectives (e.g., asking students to elaborate on their ideas, using group discussions, and delaying exposure to standard explanations or procedures). Other times, teachers may need to provide more academic structure. If students are not making sense or if what they are saying doesn't fit with the guidelines of a particular activity or task, then it is important to let students know and provide them with an opportunity to clarify their thinking. This may result in students needing to abandon an initial idea in search of more viable ones. Creativity is about both originality *and* task appropriateness. We may sometimes celebrate an interesting idea, even though we know (as in Vignette 1) that the idea isn't task appropriate (which is another way of saying it won't work). But we must also not forget task appropriateness, even if we might sometimes let errors go by (temporarily). This is one way that content standards like the Common Core and creativity can go together. Coming up with original and unusual ideas is important, but creativity also ultimately needs grounding in reality. To be truly creative one needs the domain-based skills and content knowledge represented by the Common Core. Creativity doesn't occur in a vacuum; it occurs in a domain (or several domains—interdisciplinary thinking is very creative!). It requires domain knowledge, which the Common Core attempts to address. Conversely, to acquire the skills and knowledge of the Common Core students need frequent mini-c creative insights so that they can construct clear and meaningful ways to understand and apply that content. This is what a constructivist approach to teaching and learning tells us: The best way to learn something is to think about that thing or idea in ways that allow one to construct an appropriate cognitive representation of it and to link this new or modified cognitive schema to other things one knows.

When teachers take time to encourage, listen to, and provide supportive feedback to their students, they are demonstrating that they value students' mini-c ideas (Beghetto, 2007). What is supportive feedback? Supportive feedback is feedback that has substance and focuses on improvement. Substantive feedback helps students recognize when their ideas are creative, helps them understand what specifically is creative about their ideas, and offers suggestions for how they can improve upon those ideas. When students view teacher feedback as honest and supportive, they are more likely to develop confidence in their ideas (Bandura, 1997; Beghetto, 2006).

Little-c: Everyday Creativity

With feedback from other people, practice, reflection, and growth, a person can reach the next level of creativity, little-c. Little-c is everyday creativity—something that is recognized by other people as being creative. Nearly everyone can be creative at this level; it's the creativity that is a core component of one's daily life. Examples of little-c creativity might include constructing a birdhouse made for a craft fair, using duct tape to fix a broken door, or writing a poem and reading it out loud at a coffeehouse.

In the context of the classroom, helping students develop their mini-c ideas into little-c contributions is often the goal of teaching for creativity. How might this be accomplished? One way is to create learning activities that require students to share and elaborate on their mini-c ideas. When teaching new concepts, for example, teachers can have students work in groups to come up with their own unique metaphors for those concepts. An example of this is illustrated in a grade 5 Social Studies lesson reported in Cho et al. (2013, pp. 164–165). The teacher in this example taught her students about economic activities, then had them work in small groups, asking them to use one word to finish the sentence "Economy is . . ." Students were expected to come up with their own unique metaphor based on what they had been taught. Each group came up with different metaphors and a representative from each group was asked to share her or his ideas and explanations with the entire class. The following is an excerpt from the class discussion:

> *Student (S)*: Economy is a root.
> *Teacher (T)*: A root? Why do you think it's a root? Can you give us an explanation?
> *S*: Under the tree of economy, there are roots of product, consume, and distribution. There are also small roots like resources.
> *T*: Oh, everything we've learned today is like a big tree with big roots and small roots. Excellent idea, group five! How about other groups? Group Three . . .

The teacher in the above example does three things supportive of developing mini-c ideas into little-c contributions. First, the teacher provides curricular time and space for students to work with newly learned concepts. Students are expected to take academic concepts and combine them with their mini-c ideas. Small group discussions encourage students to articulate and refine these ideas. Doing so helps students develop their capacity to use academic content as a basis for generating creative ideas.

Next, the teacher requires her students to share their ideas with the entire class. Once they do, she asks for further elaboration (e.g., "A root? Why do you think it's a root? Can you give us an explanation?"). This teacher's approach differs from the prototypical initiate-respond-evaluate pattern of classroom talk (Mehan, 1979), in which teachers immediately evaluate students' ideas (e.g., "Good job!"). Exploring first and then evaluating is a simple yet powerful way to encourage a habit of creative elaboration (Beghetto, 2013), which helps students shape their mini-c ideas into little-c contributions.

Finally, after students provide their rationale for their group's idea, the teacher provides further clarification, amplification, and validation of their ideas. The teacher once again delays evaluation. She first rearticulates the idea in a more succinct way—highlighting how it connects with the day's lesson ("Oh, everything we've learned today is like a big tree with big roots and small roots") and then evaluates the idea ("Excellent idea . . ."). In this way, other students can benefit from this novel and meaningful idea about the economy. In addition, rather than stopping with one group, the teacher continues to call on the other groups using the same elaboration-rearticulation-evaluation approach—helping to articulate additional little-c conceptions (e.g., Economy is a "circular bus," Economy is "entertainment," and so on).

This rather simple adjustment to the prototypical approach to teacher-talk can go a long way to establish a learning environment in which creative thinking is not an extracurricular add-on, but what is expected when learning new concepts. Making creativity a habit of thought (Sternberg, 2006) is what accomplished creators do all the time. The difference is that accomplished creators have become experts in their fields.

Pro-c: Professional Creativity

It takes approximately 10 years of deliberate practice to become an expert at anything (Ericsson, 1996), and creativity is no different. The next level in the Four-C model is Pro-c, or professional creativity. Just as feedback is the key component to growing from mini-c to little-c, practice is the essence of blossoming into Pro-c. The Pro-c creator is a creative expert in her or his chosen field, making notable and important contributions. Pro-c creativity is the peak that can be attained within one's own lifetime.

Big-C: Legendary Creativity

Big-C is legendary creativity—the kind of genius and eminent work that will be appreciated and remembered for centuries. One conceptualization of Big-C is Csikszentmihalyi's (1999) systems model, which presents Big-C as being at the intersection of the domain (e.g., biology), the field (e.g., journal editors or grant administrators), and the person (e.g., Gregor Mendel). It is often not possible to truly determine who is of Big-C level until many years after the person's death.

Taken together, the Four-C model represents a developmental trajectory from mini-c to Big-C. Figure 2.1, adapted from Beghetto & Kaufman (2014), illustrates how mini-c creativity serves as the starting point of later levels of creative expression. Different levels of creative expression, of course, do not always follow a linear progression. Accomplished creators may go directly from mini-c ideas to Pro-c innovations. Also, as illustrated in Figure 2.1, when students work alongside an expert companion it is possible for them to generate mini-c insights that lead to Pro-c contributions.

Consider the 6th-grade student named Gabriel Leal (reported in Lofing, 2009). Gabriel had a mini-c insight that pistachios might be a better bait than what has traditionally been used to control orangeworms (a major pest for nut growers in California). His insight was based on his own experiences (pistachios tasted better to him) and interpretation of the problem (if he preferred the taste of pistachios, then perhaps the orangeworms would also prefer pistachios). Although Gabriel's mini-c insight ran counter to prior practice, he was able to test his idea in a controlled experiment, under the supervision of one of his father's colleagues at a UC Davis lab. The results of the experiment surprised researchers and confirmed Gabriel's mini-c insight. Gabriel's father even reported the results at a professional conference, thereby making a Pro-C contribution.

Figure 2.1. Four-C Developmental Trajectory

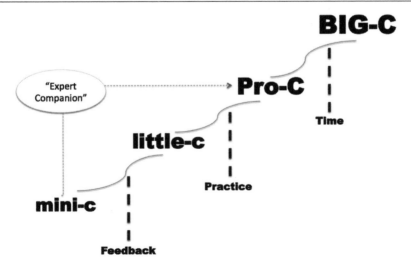

In most cases, however, one's ability to make higher levels of creative contributions progresses from mini-c to little-c and on to Pro-c. Let's use as an example Maria, a little girl who first tries to start her own company, a lemonade stand, when she is 8 years old. At this point, she is at the mini-c level of entrepreneurship. As she grows, her knowledge and sophistication will develop and she may then progress to little-c as she establishes a lawn-cutting business, perhaps one that employs several of her friends. Maria may continue to evolve and grow, refining her skills as she establishes more companies and attends business school. After she has paid her dues, she may become a successful entrepreneur and start her own company. At this point, she has reached Pro-c. If Maria is persistent, gifted, and lucky, she may eventually be considered Big-C alongside other legends of business, such as J. P. Morgan or Levi Strauss.

There are many other creativity theories that are relevant to the world of education. One is the Investment Theory of Creativity (Sternberg & Lubart, 1995). This theory is rooted in the metaphor of investment banking—the idea that creative people "buy" less appealing ideas at a low price, and then "sell" them to others after they have tinkered with them and made them more interesting. The creative person will then usually move on to the next less-desirable idea (often right as other people are jumping on the bandwagon of the previous idea). This theory drills home the point that people may need to be convinced of the power of a creative idea; indeed, some have argued that "persuasion" should be the fifth P (Simonton, 1990).

Within the Investment Theory, six constructs are proposed that enable creativity: intelligence, knowledge, thinking style, personality, motivation, and environment. If someone has a deficit in one or more of these areas, that person will likely be less creative. For example, a person who is creative in an environment that squelches their ideas will have an obstacle to overcome.

The Componential Model of Creativity (Amabile, 1996) proposes different ingredients for creativity: domain-relevant skills (such as knowledge, expertise, technical skills, and intelligence), creativity-relevant processes (such as personality, cognitive style, and propensity for risk-taking), and task motivation (an intrinsic desire to solve the problem, or finish the task). Following this model, in order for a math student to be creative, she should have domain-relevant skills (such as an understanding of algebra and geometry), creativity-relevant processes (such as a personality that is open to new experiences and willing to take risks), and task motivation (such as a passionate interest in mathematics).

You may note that Amabile makes a distinction between what is needed to be creative in a specific domain versus what is useful to be creative in general. This issue is an often-studied one in creativity research, and the Amusement Park Theoretical (APT) model (Baer & Kaufman, 2005, 2006;

Kaufman & Baer, 2004a) specifically examines this question. The APT model uses the whimsical analogy of going to an amusement park for the creative process. To go to an amusement park, there are some basic necessities, such as a ticket and method of transportation. You may then first decide on what type of park you want to visit (exciting roller-coasters or family fun), then narrow in on a specific choice (Six Flags or Knots Berry Farm), and finally, choose a particular ride (Nitro or El Toro).

The path to be creative, the APT model says, is similar. There are some specific general skills and dispositions that serve as the initial requirements for creative performance in most domains. In order to be creative (at anything), the theory argues, someone should have a certain level of intelligence, a reasonably supportive environment, and the basic motivation to create something new. Beyond these general necessities, a person is then attracted to a broad thematic area (such as science, visual arts, or the written word). The next level becomes more specific, with different themes encompassing many domains. Science could be chemistry, biology, physics, or many other fields; the written word might mean poetry, prose, plays, or journalism, among others. Finally, each domain has many microdomains; for example, a poet might write haikus or sonnets or free verse.

CREATIVITY: APPLYING THE THEORIES

We have covered several different theories and perspectives on creativity, but perhaps the most important concept is that creativity is complicated. Let's say that you want to increase creativity in the classroom (and, indeed, our hope is that you do). What exactly does that mean? Using the Four-P framework, you might think about whether you want to focus on the creative product (which might either be your lesson plans or the products your students produce), the creative person (which could lead you to think about specific qualities you might bring out in your students, such as openness to experience), the creative process (such as those used during activities in the classroom), or the creative press (such as the specific classroom environment, which may provide students with the resources needed for creativity).

Taking a different tack, you might think about the Four C's. Each level of the model has implications for the classroom. For example, being aware of mini-c creativity can bring home the point that such personal insights can grow into larger expressions of creativity. Further, even those small inspirations that are destined to blossom into a bigger idea have value and meaning in their own right. Creative expression at the mini-c level is possible for nearly every student on a daily basis across nearly any area. Indeed, Elena Grigorenko and her colleagues (Grigorenko, Jarvin, Tan, & Sternberg,

2008) propose that creativity can be woven into all aspects of learning by integrating concepts from different domains. Scientific knowledge, they suggest, can be illustrated in artistic projects or written about in stories.

Moving on to the next stage, the key to little-c creativity is feedback. We have argued elsewhere (Beghetto & Kaufman, 2007) for the Goldilocks Principle—that there is an optimal level of criticism in giving feedback. On the one hand, if feedback is delivered using standards that are unrealistically high, there is the risk of discouraging a student's creativity. On the other hand, it is just as potentially damaging to offer a response that overpraises. A student who is repeatedly reinforced for poor performance will not learn to grow. There is no magic formula; the balance between being too harsh or too lax is as delicate a tightrope as Goldilocks negotiating the firmness of an ursine mattress.

Beghetto (2005) has suggested a number of specific recommendations. These include (1) setting challenging goals for students; (2) encouraging students to find the elements of an assignment that are personally relevant; (3) minimizing (as much as possible) the pressures of testing and evaluation; (4) guiding students to think of improving their performance and understanding the material instead of task completion; and (5) emphasizing learning from mistakes, as opposed to simply trying to avoid them.

Most K–12 students will not display Pro-c creativity, but it is still a relevant concept for the classroom. The Pro-c level of creativity can serve as an aspirational goal for students. Math teachers can include brief descriptions of the kinds of professional and creative work done by professionals who use mathematics. ELA teachers can similarly describe how professionals creatively use skills and knowledge represented in students' ELA courses. Providing students with the opportunity to interact with professionals is perhaps one of the most powerful ways to inspire students' Pro-c goals and aspirations. This can include inviting visits from local architects, statisticians, plumbers, novelists, newspaper editors, builders, or any professional that puts mathematical and ELA knowledge to creative use. More surprising examples are the ideal (e.g., how an artist uses mathematics in her abstract paintings). The key is to provide opportunities for students to hear firsthand what it takes to use math and ELA creatively in and across various professions and academic disciplines. This includes learning about everything from the type and amount of professional training required to how creativity is judged in that particular profession. Providing students with opportunities to interact with Pro-c professionals (directly and through the use of classroom-based technology like Skype or Google Hangouts) can go a long way in sparking and sustaining students' interest in and understanding of how creativity can be expressed using mathematics and ELA.

If Pro-c creativity is a goal with measurable steps and markers, then Big-C creativity can serve as an inspiration. Legendary geniuses can illustrate the peak of creative heights that have been shown across different domains. Beyond that, by delving into the life stories of great creators, you can highlight their developmental trajectories. Mark Twain, Marie Curie, and Winston Churchill did not spontaneously achieve greatness—they grew into their genius, advancing through creative trajectories that include the same steps your students are climbing. Steve Jobs and Steven Spielberg had their share of surprising discoveries, noble failures, and arduous hours of hard work.

CREATIVITY: MISPERCEPTIONS

Simply knowing the basics about creativity gives you a leg up on most people. Indeed, many people may hold unconscious biases against creativity! In a recent study, Mueller, Melwani, and Goncalo (2012) looked at people's attitudes toward creativity—both explicit (what they might say) and implicit (what they might feel). People did not say they had bad feelings about creativity. But the researchers were also able to look at how people felt by using a measurement device called the Implicit Attitudes Test. This technique measures a person's reaction time in connecting two ideas. Broadly speaking, the quicker the response, the closer the person holds these two ideas together in their head (Greenwald & Banaji, 1995). So, for example, let's say that you love French fries and you hate carrots. You would be quicker to associate "French fries" and "terrific" than you would associate "French fries" and "yuck," even though the directions for the task might instruct one to make such associations. So what did people actually think about creativity? It depended on their tolerance for ambiguity. Just like being open to new experiences, being able to tolerate ambiguous situations is related to creativity. If the people in the study were set up to think positively about uncertainty, then their implicit beliefs matched their explicit beliefs—in other words, what they thought was the same as what they said, which was generally no particular preference either way for creativity. However, if a person was primed to think in a negative way about uncertainty, then they showed an implicit bias against creative people regardless of what they actually reported.

These hidden negative attitudes about creativity can be found in all walks of life. Mueller, Goncalo, and Kamdar (2011), for example, found that employees did not see creative people as having strong leadership potential. Unfortunately, this phenomenon can also extend to the classroom.

A classic study by Westby and Dawson (1995) asked teachers about creative children. The teachers said they liked creative students, yet when they were asked what creativity was, they described it with words like "responsible" or "reliable." Next, the researchers asked the same teachers about how they felt about children who were impulsive, emotional, didn't know their own limitations, or would make up their own rules (all descriptors that are more related to creativity). The teachers liked these students notably less. Similar results have been found around the world (Aljughaiman & Mowrer-Reynolds, 2005; Chan & Chan, 1999; Güncer & Oral, 1993).

There's a silver lining, however, and that is the fact that you are reading this book. One of the main reasons for this bias in the classroom is that most people don't know much about creativity, and teachers are no exception. Studies have shown that creativity can come with less desirable traits. The creativity–mental illness connection is overstated (and at the mini-c or little-c level, the relationship is virtually nonexistent; see essays in Kaufman, 2014), but that doesn't mean creative kids might not be annoying. Fifty years ago, one of the legends in creativity research, E. Paul Torrance (1963), argued that teachers preferred smart students to creative ones because the smart kids were less impulsive, less disruptive, and less nonconformist.

We are not disputing that creative kids can be trying at times (indeed, we have some personal experience with this, from a number of different roles). But we would argue that the true issue is not that teachers dislike creative students—it is that there needs to be balance. One answer, we believe, is to focus on creative metacognition.

CREATIVE METACOGNITION

There is a time and place for creativity. Such a sentence feels almost sacrilegious—would there *not* be a time for creativity? Might there be a time to *stifle* creativity? Yet, if we think about the question, it is easy to think of many examples of when *not* to be creative. An airplane pilot descending on a routine landing should be as uncreative as possible unless an engine starts to fail. It is perfectly okay for the pilot to land that plane in the exact same way as her last 30 landings. What about in the case of a dentist drilling a cavity? Unless the patient is hemorrhaging blood, a purely by-the-book solution seems eminently warranted.

We believe that the situation is no different in the classroom. Creativity is usually a great thing, whether it's a by-product of an engaging discussion or a sudden student insight on a long-debated question. But there are times when basic instruction must occur, or when certain goals need to be reached. Creativity works best when it is well-suited for the current classroom context. If students (or teachers) release their creativity with no particular concern for whether the timing is right or if others are receptive, the situation becomes like a bull in a china shop. Creative students who cannot read the situation risk being labeled disruptive, unruly, or difficult.

Sammy, the student in Vignette 2 who asked interesting questions at inconvenient times, represents a tricky example of the problem of determining when creativity is appropriate in the classroom. Sammy's questions are creative and may evidence an inquiring mind—or, although creative, his questions may instead evidence a desire to interrupt the class (or a combination of the two). Sammy's teacher is right in wanting to honor Sammy's unexpected questions; her colleague's solution—having Sammy research the answers himself and then report them to the class—honors his questions (by indicating that the answers are worth reporting to the whole class) but also puts the burden on Sammy to find the answers. If he's actually interested, he can do the necessary research (and the teacher can offer to help him but not during class). If he merely wanted to interrupt the class, this is not something the teacher should reinforce (or waste class time on).

How does one know when to be creative? According to Kaufman and Beghetto (2013b), it takes *creative metacognition*, which they define as "a combination of creative self-knowledge (knowing one's own creative strengths and limitations, both within a domain and as a general trait) and contextual knowledge (knowing when, where, how, and why to be creative)" (p. 160).

Let us break down this definition a bit. The first part is being able to know your own creative strengths and limitations. One aspect of this is to know in which domain you can best express your creativity. Perhaps you are talented in the visual arts, but could not compose an original melody for all the money in the world. Maybe you are a highly creative cook and also show aptitude for creative storytelling, vocal percussion, and crocheting. Or you are a creative physicist who has trouble stringing together an original sentence. Knowing your creative profile is a tremendously useful bit of awareness.

Beyond this basic understanding of your own creativity peaks and valleys, however, it is also helpful to know how you compare with others. You might know that you're a creative historian, but are you little-c or Pro-c? If you were to write a short story, would most people consider you mini-c? Examples of people with "a disconnect" about their own abilities can be seen on television all the time. On *American Idol* and other shows of this ilk, the winners and runners-up are usually at the Pro-c level. Some people on the high end of little-c may squeak in; only time will tell if these shows truly produce a Big-C singer. Yet, when these programs first show the tryouts and competitions, they include singers who are (at best) mini-c. At these auditions, aspiring singers who are out of touch about their talent are often held up for public ridicule. Knowing their own strengths and limitations could help students (and adults) avoid such ridicule and find appropriate venues to display their talents—not to mention that it could lead them to appropriate ways to enhance their talents.

The second component of the creative metacognition definition may be even more challenging. It's not enough to know your own creativity; you also have to know the best contexts for creativity. Some environments are more creativity-supportive than others. Davies and his colleagues (2012) have identified several factors that characterize an optimally supportive learning environment. Creativity-supportive environments use space and time flexibly, provide materials that support learning and exploration, allow students to have some choice in the learning, cultivate respectful relationships among teachers and students, provide opportunities for peer collaboration, and establish meaningful partnerships with outside agencies. We recognize that this long list of features is probably more aspirational than practical, but it provides some sense of what an optimal learning environment might entail. Teachers who support students' creativity recognize that they need not provide all of the features of an optimal learning environment. Indeed, all teachers can find ways to blend some of these features, at least some of the time, into their classrooms. They can then help their students recognize when and in what context creative expression might be appropriate and welcomed.

For instance, students who are just learning a mathematical procedure or writing style might benefit from copying an existing model. Once they understand the procedure or style, they can then try to put their own twist on it. The first phase of instruction might be more direct and prescriptive. This can then be followed by a more exploratory and student-directed approach, wherein students can try making their own alternations or modifications to an approach or style. Other times, teachers may choose to flip this order. They could have students explore first, then provide a more structured model. Either way, the key for teachers is helping students develop the contextual knowledge necessary for deciding when direct replication or creative alteration is most appropriate.

A different kind of example of learning in which context creative expression might be appropriate and welcome also comes from Vignette 2. If Sammy's teacher followed the advice of the colleague who suggested having Sammy research his own somewhat-off-topic questions, Sammy might not only learn the answers to those questions but also something about when it is appropriate to pose certain kinds of questions, which is an aspect of creative metacognition. As a more extreme example, imagine a student who finds creative ways to disrupt class every day. (Sadly, this is not very hard to imagine—it happens all the time.) A teacher who can help this student learn that creative disruptions are unwelcome and who can also show the student how to use those creative impulses and ideas in more appropriate ways will provide an enormous benefit to the student (as well as herself and the rest of the class, which won't be constantly interrupted!).

FROM CONCEPTS TO CLASSROOM

1. ***Creativity is more than originality.*** One of the most common roadblocks to incorporating creativity in the classroom is the belief that creativity is the same thing as originality. If creativity is thought of as simply a form of originality, then it is easy to imagine how it could quickly spiral out of control. When this happens, creativity competes with academic learning. Fortunately, as we have described, creativity is the combination of originality *and* task appropriateness. One way to think about this is to view students as providing the originality, and the academic subject matter as providing the task-appropriate constraints. In this way, creativity and academic subject matter work together.

2. ***There are different levels of creativity.*** Another common roadblock results from believing that only highly accomplished people are creative. The Four-C model helps broaden one's conception of creativity. In the context of the classroom, mini-c and little-c creativity will be most relevant. Teachers can therefore focus their attention on helping students develop their mini-c ideas into meaningful little-c contributions. Larger C examples can still play a role, but more as an aspirational goal. Students can learn about highly accomplished creators in various academic domains as part of their own smaller-c learning and development.

3. ***Successful creators know when to be creative and when not to be creative.*** Creative expression often comes with a cost. Accomplished creators weigh the costs and benefits of sharing their creative ideas. If they feel that the benefits outweigh the costs, they are more likely to share their creative ideas and products. Sometimes it's a matter of recognizing that a particular creative contribution is better suited for a different time or place. Teachers can help develop this same skill in their students by explicitly teaching the kinds of self-knowledge and contextual-knowledge necessary for making a creative contribution.

4. ***Creativity needs the kinds of content knowledge and skills represented in the Common Core.*** Creativity isn't just originality (as noted in point 1, above). To meet the second requirement of creativity—task appropriateness—students will need the kinds of knowledge outlined in the Common Core. To be creative at the little-c, Pro-c, or Big-C levels requires increasingly sophisticated kinds of domain knowledge. Creativity doesn't occur in a vacuum—it also needs the "stuff" of content.

5. ***Developing the skills and learning the content of the Common Core will require mini-c creativity on a daily basis.*** Constructivist models of learning have shown us that to understand an idea one must

construct its meaning as an internal representation that is linked to other cognitive constructs. That means taking the raw material of experience (including all the kinds of classroom experiences a student might have) and turning those into cognitive schemata. Students need to *think* about the content and to *create* those cognitive representations and links.

CONCLUDING THOUGHTS

There are those who have suggested that the Common Core stifles creativity (Egan, 2014), but this shows a fundamental misunderstanding of how creativity works. Egan argued that creativity requires "messiness and magic, serendipity and insanity"—all of which may be true, but none of which makes the case that the content knowledge and skills called for in the Common Core are not *also* needed for creativity. Creativity *does* require originality, novelty, unusual ideas, and perhaps even "messiness and magic, serendipity and insanity," at least sometimes (although the insanity connection has been overblown in the popular press—see Kaufman, 2014). But creativity also requires knowing a great deal about the domain(s) in which one is working.

None of the theories described in this chapter—and none of the major theories of creativity being espoused by creativity experts today—denies the importance of knowledge for creativity. To be creative at the highest levels—Big-C creativity—requires so much domain expertise that creativity researchers have argued for a "10-year rule" that posits a requirement of at least 10 years working, studying, practicing, and experimenting in a domain before anyone can make the kind of paradigm-shifting creative contributions that we call genius. Creativity at lower levels also requires domain knowledge, albeit less extensive expertise. In fact, as a general rule, higher levels of creativity require higher levels of domain knowledge and skill. There is a solid positive correlation between the two.

This is not to say that domain knowledge or expertise are the same as creativity, however. One can have a great deal of domain knowledge without evidencing comparable levels of creativity. There is a positive correlation. The most creative people in a field will necessarily have strong skills and extensive knowledge of that field; however, there may well be others in their field who are less creative, yet have even more extensive expertise. To set the two at odds, however, and to suggest that promoting one means necessarily demoting the other, is simply wrong. It is also damaging, because it leads to false choices in education.

Expectations of what students should know and be able to do—the kinds of things outlined in the Common Core, and in all the various state standards that the Common Core State Standards are replacing—*can* cause teachers who mistakenly believe those standards are at odds with other things (like creativity) to neglect those other things. This is true even if attending to those other things might actually help students meet the expectations of the standards, as is the case with creativity. We have shown that not only is content knowledge necessary for creativity, but that creativity can help students acquire content knowledge. It is only a dogmatic insistence that it must be one or the other, but never both, which gets in the way of the many synergies available.

Consider this analogy: One could argue that there are a limited number of hours in the school day, and therefore time spent studying mathematics necessarily takes away from time that could be spent studying science. Based on this premise, one could maintain that studying mathematics must hinder the learning of science, and to promote science learning one must spend less time teaching math. Does that make sense? Of course not. One needs mathematics to learn many things in science, and learning both math and science can result in more knowledge and understanding of both subjects, not less.

So it is with creativity and the kind of content knowledge and skills that the Common Core represents. One can force them to be at odds with each other, just as one can force math and science to compete for class time, but that would be foolish. There are many ways in which promoting one can promote the other. That is what the next several chapters will be showing you how to do!

CHAPTER 3

Learning Environments that Support Creativity and the Common Core

---

Vignette 1: Math Motorcycles

A 2nd-grade teacher starts each year reviewing basic math facts with her students. In alignment with the domain of Operations and Algebraic Thinking of the Common Core State Standards, she knows that students entering 2nd grade should be able to demonstrate fluency for addition and subtraction within 10. Of course, some of her students have yet to attain fluency and all of her students could use a bit more practice. In the past she used timed worksheets—asking her students to complete as many addition and subtraction problems in 2 minutes as they could. This activity was often met with groans. This year she decided to come up with a more "creative" practice activity. Why not turn practice worksheets into a game: Math Motorcycles. She cut out paper motorcycles, asked her students to personalize them, and hung them on the wall above the board on a "racetrack." All 22 motorcycles were lined up at the "starting line" and each time a student accurately completed the problems on the worksheet, the motorcycles would advance one step closer to the finish line. The first one across the finish line earned a "big prize" from the prize box and each subsequent one across the finish line would get a "smaller prize." Her students, upon hearing her explain these rules, were thrilled! In 20 years of teaching she never before witnessed such enthusiasm to start working on math worksheets. What do you think of this activity? Is it creative? Is it motivating to students? Will such a lesson help students practice their math facts? Do you see any problems or potential negative consequences with this approach? We will return to this example and address these questions later in the chapter.

Vignette 2: Reading Ratatouille

A 7th-grade teacher was concerned about his incoming students' limited proficiency in reading and comprehending a wide range of literature (e.g., stories, dramas, poems, and informational texts). Recognizing that developing this proficiency is a key Common Core reading standard for his grade level, he decided to come up with a way to motivate his students by creating a reading reward program called Reading Ratatouille. Just as a ratatouille dish is a beautiful combination of different vegetables, reading ratatouille requires students to read different types of literature. Students are asked to read a story, drama, poem, and informational text from an assigned list (each progressively more difficult); they then take an online quiz. Once they have completed a total of four assigned texts (i.e., a selection from each type of literature) and demonstrated proficiency in comprehension on each (i.e., passed the comprehension quiz at 80% or higher), they earn a free pass to the monthly pizza party hosted by a local pizzeria. The pizzeria donated a buffet that included favorite and special orders from the class (e.g., gluten-free offerings, vegan pizzas, etc.). This teacher's students couldn't wait to start reading once they heard him describe it. What do you think of this teacher's reading program? Is it creative? Is it motivating to students? Will such a lesson help students improve their reading skills? Do you see any problems or potential negative consequences with this approach? We will return to this example and address these questions later in the chapter.

ESTABLISHING A SUPPORTIVE LEARNING ENVIRONMENT

How can teachers combine creativity and the Common Core State Standards? The first step is developing a learning environment that is supportive of both creativity and standards-based learning. At first blush, cultivating creativity and standards-based learning may seem like opposing or, at the very least, different curricular goals. But, as we have discussed, once we get beyond common misconceptions about creativity, we can see that creativity and content standards can be complementary.

Creativity in the classroom is a form of constrained originality (Beghetto, 2013). The Common Core State Standards provide the context (or constraints) within which students and teachers can develop their original thinking, behavior, and products. But even when we understand how creativity can (and often does) thrive in the context of content standards, we can still inadvertently stifle student creativity. Is this because content standards can be too limiting and too constraining? We would say no.

It is not content standards by themselves that stifle creativity. In fact, in the Common Core State Standards for Mathematics, it is plainly stated that "these Standards do not dictate curriculum or teaching methods" (NGACPB & CCSSO, 2014c, p. 5). Indeed, teachers who teach using the Common Core can still choose whatever curricular approaches or teaching methods they want—including creative approaches. If standards aren't the reason why student creativity is stifled, then are we simply blaming teachers? Not at all. We firmly believe that creativity is not willfully stifled by teachers. Collectively, the three of us have worked with and taught many thousands of prospective and practicing teachers. We have never come across even a single teacher who has expressed a stated goal of stifling students' creativity. It is often just the opposite. Many teachers go into teaching because they envision it as a profession that will allow them to express their own instructional creativity and provide them with an opportunity to support the creative learning and expression of their students.

How, then, does creativity get suppressed? We would argue that much of the reason why student *and* teacher creativity is stifled in schools and classrooms is a result of the policies, practices, and procedures of the learning environment. More specifically, whether creativity will be supported or suppressed depends to a great extent on how teachers and students experience the motivational messages that are sent by their particular teaching and learning environment (Beghetto, 2013; Beghetto & Kaufman, 2014). Many common instructional practices inadvertently constrain teacher and student creativity. Some of these practices are inherited from teachers' own prior schooling experiences, and others emerge out of teachers' well-intended efforts to motivate student engagement. In this chapter, we will discuss common practices that have been found to spur creativity and highlight how teachers can avoid policies, practices, and procedures that tend to kill, or at least suppress, the motivation necessary for creativity (Amabile, 1996; Hennessey, 2010a).

What Role Does Motivation Play in Learning and Creative Expression?

Every teacher knows that learning depends on students putting forth effort and engaging with what is being taught. Teachers also know that some students seem more willing to put forth and sustain effort than others. Some students already have interest in what is being taught; others have little or no interest. Some students are motivated and ready to learn; others are not. There are many ways that teachers can and do try to motivate students to learn (recall the two opening vignettes), some that can be effective in the short run and some that can have unanticipated negative outcomes, such as stifling creativity. If teachers have a deeper understanding of the role that motivation plays in their classroom they will be in a better position to promote the kinds of task engagement that also support students' meaningful learning and creativity.

What is motivation? The word *motivation* is derived from the Latin word *movere*, which literally means *to move*. In the context of the classroom, student motivation refers to the reason why students do something. Although there are many reasons why students engage (or do not engage) in learning tasks, motivational researchers (Ryan & Deci, 2000) have proposed the following three categories:

First, students who engage in learning tasks because they find them interesting, satisfying, and enjoyable are said to be *intrinsically* motivated. Second, students who engage in a task for external reasons such as pleasing others, avoiding punishment, or gaining some external reward or recognition are said to be *extrinsically* motivated. Finally, if students have no reason to engage in a task, then they are said to be *amotivated*. Amotivated students avoid or refuse to engage in learning tasks because they see no point in doing so. Let's start by taking a closer look at intrinsic motivation.

Why Is Intrinsic Motivation Important?

Creativity and learning thrive under conditions of intrinsic motivation (Hennessey, 2010b). Intrinsically motivated students do not need external reasons for engaging in the tasks that they find interesting and enjoyable (Amabile, Hill, Hennessey, & Tighe, 1994). They seek out tasks that interest them, engage in these tasks for the enjoyment that such tasks provide, and challenge themselves so they can continue to develop their skills and competence. Sometimes our efforts to motivate students can inadvertently result in undermining their intrinsic motivation. Indeed, it is our best motivational intentions that can sometimes pave the path to lower levels of student engagement, learning, and creative expression. In what follows we take a closer look at the well-intended motivational activities from the two opening vignettes and explore how features of these two activities can undermine students' intrinsic motivation.

Revisiting Reading Ratatouille. Let's return to the 7th-grade teacher's Reading Ratatouille idea described above in Vignette 2. Although establishing a reward contingency (i.e., a pass to the pizza party) for reading various books can initially increase students' interest in wanting to read, in the long run it can undermine students' existing intrinsic interest and, in turn, negatively influence student learning and creativity. Why might this be the case?

Consider students who already enjoy reading various types of texts. They read because they enjoy it, and they find it satisfying and interesting.

By introducing a new reason for reading—the reward of a pizza party—students who read for fun may now replace that internal reason with this new external reason. Something that was once fun now becomes work. Reading is no longer an enjoyable end in itself, but rather a means to another end. A clear sign that this has happened is when students start asking, "What will I get if I do this?"

There is a long line of research consistently demonstrating the tendency for expected reward to have a detrimental effect on students' intrinsic motivation and creativity (Amabile, 1996). Extrinsic constraints like rewards or anticipated evaluations can have the unanticipated negative result of driving out intrinsic motivation, and creativity tends to be associated with intrinsic, not extrinsic, motivation. Increasing motivation through the use of rewards therefore tends to decrease creativity, and it can have long-term negative consequences for student interest, engagement, and learning. Increasing extrinsic motivation can sometimes have a short-term positive impact on task motivation but at the same time undermine longer-term intrinsic motivation. Students may do the activity to earn the reward or the good evaluation but lose interest in doing the activity, even an activity that they once enjoyed, after the reward is no longer available.

Kruglanski, Friedman, and Zeevi (1971) conducted one of the earliest studies that demonstrated how being promised a reward could reduce students' enjoyment and creativity as compared to students who did not expect to receive a reward. Since that time, researchers have continued to demonstrate how extrinsic rewards can undermine quality performance and creativity (Amabile, 1983, 1996; Baer, 1997, 1998; Hennessey & Amabile, 1988; Lepper & Greene, 1975, 1978). Hennessey (2010b), for example, has explained that across "hundreds of published investigations . . . the promise of reward made contingent on task engagement often serves to undermine intrinsic task motivation and qualitative aspects of performance, including creativity . . . this effect is so robust that it has been found to occur across a wide age range with everyone from preschoolers to seasoned business professionals" (p. 345).

One reason why this happens is because students can become focused on obtaining the reward rather than on engaging deeply and meaningfully with the task. In the case of the reading example, if a pizza-party reward is also contingent on obtaining a high score on the reading comprehension quiz, then students may be less likely to take the risk of focusing on their own interpretations or ideas about what they are reading. Instead, they may realize that the best way to obtain the reward is to converge on the expected answer, even if they don't agree with it or fully understand it. Focusing on preexisting responses, rather than meaningfully engaging with and developing one's own interpretations of texts undermines both meaningful understanding and creativity.

A focus on the reward, rather than on the learning task, can also undermine the type of learning that is described in the Common Core State Standards. In fact, the ELA Common Core State Standards explicitly state, "Students who meet the Standards *readily undertake* the close, attentive reading that is at the heart of *understanding and enjoying* complex works of literature. . . . They *actively seek the wide, deep, and thoughtful engagement* with high-quality literary and informational texts . . . " (NGACPB & CCSSO, 2014b, p. 3, italics added). The descriptors we italicized are the same descriptors of intrinsically motivated students. Students who are intrinsically motivated "readily undertake" complex tasks; at the heart of their engagement is a focus on "understanding and enjoying" the tasks; and they "actively seek" out opportunities for "wide, deep, and thoughtful engagement" in what interests them.

Of course, not all students will suffer negative effects on learning and creativity from extrinsic rewards. Some students can indeed be meaningfully motivated by rewards. Researchers such as Eisenberger and his colleagues (Eisenberger, Pierce, & Cameron, 1999; Eisenberger & Shanock, 2003) have provided evidence that clearly targeted rewards, paired with direct instructions to be creative, can have no negative effect and can even enhance creativity. In adults, the relationship can be even stronger; Byron and Khazanchi (2012) conducted a meta-analysis of many different studies and found that rewards increased creativity if the rewards were specifically contingent on creative performance.

One explanation for this is to understand that not everyone experiences extrinsic motivators in the same way. For example, the idea of prosocial motivation, as outlined by Forgeard and Mecklenburg (2013), integrates the idea of intrinsic versus extrinsic motivation with the notion of audience. Just as people can be motivated by intrinsic or extrinsic factors, so too can they be motivated by self or others. Intrinsic self-oriented motivation, which Forgeard and Mecklenburg call "Growth," is rooted in the personal enjoyment of the creative task itself. Intrinsic other-oriented motivation, which is called "Guidance," is probably the closest to what teachers strive for—the joy of sharing one's gifts to help others experience the same rush. Extrinsic self-oriented motivation "Gain" is the standard motivation derived from wanting extra credit, praise, or financial incentives. Finally, extrinsic other-oriented motivation, "Giving," is using the specific manifestations of your creativity to help others. It is still extrinsic motivation because there is a tangible, manifest outcome that drives you, but it is focused on helping others.

As we will discuss later in this chapter, there are different types of extrinsic motivators (Ryan & Deci, 2000). Some tend to have more detrimental effects on task engagement than others. In fact, it is possible to use extrinsic motivators in ways that can yield positive outcomes similar to

intrinsic motivation. Prior to elaborating on these different types and experiences of extrinsic motivation, it is safe to say that, in general, engaging in
tasks for the purpose of attaining external rewards tends to undermine the
kinds of meaningful engagement and creativity that most teachers strive for
in their classrooms. Consequently, teachers should be careful how they use
rewards so they do not inadvertently undermine students' joy and passion
for learning and their willingness to take the risks necessary for creative
thought and expression.

In addition to expected rewards, there are several other extrinsic motivators and motivational messages that can inadvertently undermine student
learning and creativity. Let's revisit the Math Motorcycles activity, described
in Vignette 1 above, to explore how features of this activity can also inadvertently undermine intrinsic motivation.

Revisiting Math Motorcycles. The teacher in this vignette wanted to transform the practice of math facts into a game. After describing the activity to
her students, they all seemed eager to engage. If we were to fast-forward a
few days or weeks, however, would we see the same level of engagement in
the activity? Probably not. At least not for all students. Although the teacher
designed this activity to make practice exercises more engaging and enjoyable for her students, it can—somewhat paradoxically—undermine student
interest and creativity. One reason, as described above, is because the activity focuses students' attention on expected rewards. In addition to rewards,
the activity also uses externally imposed time constraints, makes evaluation salient, and emphasizes competition. These features of the activity send
messages to students that can undermine motivation, learning, and creative
expression (Amabile, 1996; Hennessey, 2010a; Midgley, 2002).

Let's start with time constraints. Why might time constraints have a
negative effect on student motivation, learning, and creative expression?
One reason, much as we discussed in the Reading Ratatouille example, is
that time constraints focus students' attention on completing the task rather
than spending the necessary time to achieve meaningful engagement with the
task. Amabile and her colleagues (Amabile, DeJong, & Lepper, 1976), for
example, demonstrated that deadlines for completing a word game had an
adverse effect on participants' intrinsic interest in the game (as compared to
participants who finished the task but did not face such deadlines).

In the case of the motorcycle math activity, students may feel that the
most important goal of the activity is to quickly converge on correct answers. Indeed, this is the only way students' motorcycles can advance toward the finish line. Even though the teacher intended for this activity to be
fun and more like a game, the pressure to correctly finish their worksheets

in an allotted amount of time can—somewhat ironically—result in students experiencing this activity as more test-like. When this happens, students are less likely to take the types of intellectual risks that are supportive of meaningful learning and creativity (Beghetto, 2009; Clifford, 1991).

In addition to the imposed time constraints, two of the most problematic aspects of the motorcycle activity are that it emphasizes expected evaluation and social comparison among students—both of which have been found to be detrimental to creativity (Amabile, 1979, 1982; Amabile, Goldfarb, & Brackfield, 1990) and student learning (Ames, 1992; Midgley, 2002). Indeed, as Hennessey (2010b) has explained, "The expectation that one's work will be judged and compared . . . may well be the most deleterious extrinsic constraint of all [because] competition often combines aspects of other 'killers' of motivation and creativity, including expected reward and expected evaluation" (p. 348).

Consequently, students may be less likely to share their own unique and personally meaningful (or mini-c) ideas for how they arrived at their solutions (Beghetto & Kaufman, 2007). Moreover, because student progress is displayed in a highly visible fashion (i.e., the math motorcycles are posted above the front chalkboard), students who may have difficulty completing the worksheet during the allotted time may develop a performance-avoidant orientation toward math (Ames, 1992; Midgley, 2002). When students adopt a performance-avoidant orientation, they are motivated to avoid the appearance of incompetence in the eyes of their teachers or peers (Midgley, 2002). Performance-avoidant students tend to engage in various maladaptive learning behaviors, including avoiding help when needed, withdrawing effort, making public excuses for potentially negative performance in advance of engaging in tasks, and cheating (Maehr & Midgley, 1996).

The motorcycle math activity, when viewed through the lens of prior theory and research on motivation, represents a potentially detrimental blend of extrinsic motivators and motivational messages. Regardless of the fact that the teacher intended the motorcycle math activity to be experienced by her students as enjoyable and engaging, it is likely that some of her students will experience this activity as demotivating—undermining their willingness to take the risks necessary for creative learning and expression. Even those who may be motivated by it (typically more successful students who earn more rewards in such an activity) may have their long-term intrinsic motivation for math decreased as a result of participating in this rewards-based game. In this way, an activity that seems to be engaging and exciting may actually result in the inadvertent suppression of intrinsic motivation, creative expression, and meaningful standards-based learning.

FROM CONCEPTS TO CLASSROOM

How Can Teachers Protect Intrinsic Motivation?

Thus far we have discussed ways in which teachers might inadvertently undermine students' intrinsic motivation. The question that many teachers might have at this point is: What can I do to protect and support my students' intrinsic motivation? Fortunately, there are several things that teachers can do. As we have discussed elsewhere (Kaufman, Beghetto, & Baer, 2010), we can support students' intrinsic motivation by expressing interest in students' ideas, projects, and activities. It is also helpful to talk to them and listen to them talk about their interests, and then provide opportunities and resources (books, projects, materials, information, websites) with which they can pursue their interests when appropriate. But we want to be careful that we don't inadvertently replace students' existing interest and enjoyment with engaging in tasks for external reasons, such as rewards or even our approval.

It is also important to keep in mind that although we can help support or catalyze intrinsic motivation, we cannot force students to be intrinsically motivated. You can't make someone like something. In fact, as illustrated in the above vignettes, when we intervene too much, we run the risk of undermining preexisting intrinsic interests. Returning to the vignettes, there are a few slight changes that the teachers could have made to the activities. The 7th-grade teacher could have a monthly reading celebration in which students eat pizza and take turns discussing their favorite texts from the various genres they read (i.e., what they enjoyed most and why). Most important, participating in the celebration would not be made contingent upon reading quiz scores or on the number of texts read. Similarly, the Math Motorcycles activity could encourage students not just to come up with correct answers in the allotted time, but rather to focus on coming up with approaches to solving the problems in as many different ways as they could. Also, rather than emphasize social comparison and competition, the students could keep their own personal track record, whereby they focus on improvement, thus competing with themselves rather than worrying about how they measure up to other students in the class.

In addition to these suggestions, there are several ways that teachers might protect their students' intrinsic motivation from the potentially negative effects of extrinsic features of the classroom (adapted from suggestions described in Beghetto, 2013, pp. 111–112; Hennessey, 2010a, p. 345):

- *Incorporate student interests.* One of the most important things teachers can do is learn about their students' interests and whenever possible incorporate those interests in learning activities and assignments. How might teachers learn about students' interests? At the elementary school level, teachers can use a "student of the week" bulletin board that provides a way for students to showcase their interests—everything from favorite foods and books to favorite activities and pastimes. At higher grade levels, teachers can have their students fill out a brief information card at the beginning of the course, noting their likes and interests. Teachers can also periodically check in with their students. Whenever they discover that their students are finding a lesson or activity interesting, they may wish to be particularly careful about using extrinsic motivators. For example, they might try to minimize evaluative pressure and avoid social comparisons of progress (focusing instead on comparing current student progress with the student's own prior level of achievement).
- *Encourage intrinsic engagement.* Teachers can encourage intrinsic engagement by providing options and opportunities to include students' interests in activities and tasks and also support them in taking reasonable risks, trying out new things, and challenging themselves. When students do show engagement and improvement, help them focus on taking pride in the effort they put into their learning tasks and assignments rather than focus on external indicators of success or recognition (i.e., grades, praise from teachers and parents). Carol Dweck (2006) has shown in a variety of ingenious studies that complimenting students on their effort ("You must have worked really hard") has a positive impact on their motivation (leading them to work on projects longer and choose to take on more challenging learning activities). In contrast, complimenting students on their intellectual abilities ("You are so good at this—you must be so smart!") tends to focus students' attention on grades, reduce their interest in learning tasks, and lead them to choose less challenging tasks so that they can more easily "look smart." We want students to think of learning as something they can accomplish through effort, not something that will simply happen if they are "smart" (and not happen if they are "not smart").
- *Monitor the use of extrinsic motivators.* Realistically speaking, it is probably impossible to eliminate all extrinsic motivators from the classroom. Focus, instead, on how much and how often such motivators are used in your classroom. Take time to periodically review

and reflect on the types of incentives you use in your classroom to motivate students. Reflect on the instructions you give to students and reasons you provide when asking them to engage in learning tasks. Ask yourself questions such as: Do I focus on extrinsic incentives (or punishments) when attempting to engage students? Do I use too many extrinsic motivators? Am I using rewards where they are not needed, when students are already intrinsically motivated (and by doing so undermining their intrinsic motivation)? How might I better balance my use of extrinsic motivators with more intrinsically interesting and engaging options and tasks? What would this look like? How might I help students focus on the enjoyable and personally meaningful aspects of a particular learning task?

- *Provide students with opportunities to take control of their own learning.* When students are intrinsically motivated, they feel connected to what they are doing and feel in control of their learning (Ryan & Deci, 2000). It is, therefore, important to create a classroom atmosphere that allows students to take charge of their learning process. Avoid trying to motivate students through coercion (e.g., "You need to do this or you will fail") and contingencies (e.g., "Complete this assignment and then you'll get free time"). Instead, provide students with opportunities to develop a sense of self-initiation, participation, and direction in their learning. This can include everything from soliciting students' ideas for a class field trip or project to allowing students to come up with their own topics and goals for activities and tasks. Doing so will help students recognize that their interests and mini-c ideas can serve as the origins of their learning, rather than feeling like "pawns" (Hennessey, 2010a) in someone else's learning goals and agenda.

Teachers can help support and protect their students' intrinsic interests and enjoyment of learning by keeping the above in mind. When students find that what they are doing is interesting and engaging, they are more likely to take the risks necessary for creative thinking. Of course, not everything we ask students to do will be interesting or enjoyable. It is often the case that only a handful of students will be intrinsically motivated by any particular task. We recognize that many tasks in school (and life) that are necessary for the development of knowledge and creative competence are not, in and of themselves, intrinsically interesting. In such situations, extrinsic motivators may need to be used. So the question becomes, Can extrinsic motivators be used in a way that doesn't undermine learning and creativity? We address this question in the following section.

Can Extrinsic Motivators Be Used More Effectively?

People sometimes view intrinsic and extrinsic motivators as opposite ends of a continuum. Motivational researchers take a more nuanced view. Ryan and Deci (2000), for example, have demonstrated that there are different types and uses of extrinsic motivators—ways that can, in fact, promote students' active and self-directed learning and engagement. How might this be accomplished? One way is to make sure that teachers help students understand the rationale for engaging in tasks that are not intrinsically motivating. If students can endorse or see the value in doing such tasks—as opposed to viewing those tasks and goals as externally imposed and of little value—then it is possible to support high levels of engagement.

In short, the key is to help ensure that students experience the tasks as supporting their *autonomy* rather than as controlling their learning (Reeve, 2009; Ryan & Deci, 2000). When teachers support students' autonomy, students can see the value in learning tasks and activities and they may endorse them. Moreover, when students' autonomy is supported they are more likely to experience learning tasks with similar levels of intrinsic motivation (Ryan & Deci 2000), which in turn supports their willingness to express their creativity (Hennessey, 2010a). Conversely, when teachers fail to provide a meaningful rationale and instead use pressure, guilt, or coercion to motivate students, students will experience learning tasks as controlling.

How might you support student autonomy in your classroom? There are several ways. Below are some suggestions (adapted from recommendations presented in Beghetto, 2013, pp. 113–114; Reeve, 2009, pp. 160–162; Ryan & Deci, 2006).

- *Provide reasons for requests.* Providing meaningful rationales for why we ask students to engage in learning tasks is, arguably, one of the easiest and most effective ways of supporting student autonomy. When we make instructional requests of students—particularly when students do not feel those requests are inherently interesting—teachers can increase the chances that students endorse such requests if an explanation or reason is provided (Reeve, 2009). Imagine a high school writing class wherein one of the final assignment options is to submit a poem, short story, or essay to a local literary magazine. Students in the class are more likely to experience a teacher's request to revise their writing as autonomy-supportive if the request is accompanied by a rationale that the student can understand (". . . because you want to submit your essay to the literary magazine and it needs a bit more work before it is ready") as compared to a request that is stated as an ultimatum (e.g., "Revise it or you'll fail the assignment") or that utilizes guilt-inducing language (e.g., "If you submit it 'as is,' you'll end up embarrassing me, yourself, and the entire school"). By taking a few extra moments to provide a meaningful rationale for our instructional requests, we can increase the chances that students experience our requests as supporting their autonomy rather than as being controlling or coercive.

- *Acknowledge and incorporate students' perspectives.* Teachers have a professional responsibility to design learning tasks and help guide student learning. Sometimes it is easy to lose sight of the fact that our students also play a key role in this process. No student arrives at our classroom door void of prior experiences and perspectives. As such, one way that teachers can support student autonomy is to work on striking a better balance between our instructional responsibility to guide instruction and our students' experiences and perspectives. This requires taking the time to listen to our students and, when appropriate, integrating their ideas, perspectives, experiences, and interests into our lessons, activities, and learning tasks. As Reeve (2009) has explained, when teachers take the time to incorporate students' experiences and perspectives into their classroom activities, they are able to "create classroom conditions in which students' autonomous motivations align with their classroom activity" (p. 162). As a result, students will be more likely to endorse the learning activities, tasks, and experiences created by their teachers.

- *Provide students with meaningful options and choices.* Choices increase the chances that students can find an option that they can endorse (Reeve, 2009). Teachers can provide options to students on the types of tasks they can complete and even how they might complete them (e.g., "Pick three from the following list," "Write a persuasive essay on a topic of your choice," "Come up with your own way to solve this mathematical problem"). Importantly, offering choices does not guarantee that students will view the activity as supportive of their autonomy. Indeed, it's not simply the total number of options provided, but how students experience those options. As Ryan and Deci (2006) have explained, "One can have many options and not feel autonomy, but instead feel overwhelmed and resentful at the effort entailed in the decision making . . . one could have only one option . . . and yet feel quite autonomous so long as one truly endorses that option" (p. 1577). One way that teachers can try to support student autonomy, therefore, is to provide choices and options *and* monitor how their students experience those options. Further, there may be an interaction with culture. Although having choice is traditionally associated with increased intrinsic motivation (Kyllonen, Walters, & Kaufman, 2005), Iyengar and Lepper (1999) found that personal choice may be less related to motivation in Asian culture than in Western culture. It is important to keep these variables in mind.

- *Welcome students' thoughts, feelings, and actions.* As we have discussed, students will not always find our instructional activities and assignments interesting and engaging. There are even times when students might get upset, angry, and frustrated by the assignments and learning tasks we ask them to complete. Students, like all humans, are emotional beings. Moreover, learning is shot through with emotion (Rosiek & Beghetto, 2009)—including negative emotions. We recognize that negative student emotions are not always easy to navigate. If, however, we deny our students their emotional expression while learning, they are likely to feel controlled rather than supported. Autonomy-supportive teachers recognize that students respond in various ways to what they are learning and, therefore, anticipate and are willing to work with students' emotional responses rather than pressure or coerce them to think, feel, and act in certain ways (Reeve, 2009). Imagine a student who is frustrated by being asked to redo an assignment. An autonomy supportive teacher might respond to this student by acknowledging the frustration ("I can see that you are frustrated and understand why you don't want to redo this assignment . . . ") and provide a rationale for the request (" . . . the reason I asked you to redo this assignment . . . "), rather than simply dismiss the student's frustration out of hand (e.g., "Stop your complaining and get to work."). Autonomy-supportive teachers take the extra time to demonstrate encouragement, be patient, and listen to their students. They assess student complaints as valid and thereby increase the chances that their students will see them as supportive (Reeve, 2009).

The above suggestions, taken together, provide concrete ideas for how teachers can establish an autonomy-supportive learning environment. When teachers take such small extra steps to support student autonomy—particularly when asking students to engage in instructional tasks and activities that students may not find inherently interesting or enjoyable—they increase the likelihood that their students will be willing to engage more meaningfully with standards-based content and take the risks necessary for creative expression.

Environments that support autonomy and intrinsic motivation also promote a wide array of adaptive learning behaviors, including self-determination, curiosity, sustained engagement, positive emotions, positive self-worth, optimal challenge seeking, deeper understanding, self-regulated learning, better academic performance, and general well-being (see Hennessey, 2010b; Ryan & Deci, 2000; Reeve, 2009).

CONCLUDING THOUGHTS

The learning environment plays a non-trivial role when it comes to supporting standards-based learning and creativity simultaneously. Under the right conditions, student learning and creativity can thrive in a standards-based learning environment. The practices, policies, and procedures of the classroom send messages that communicate—often inadvertently—reasons why students should engage in learning activities and tasks. These messages are sometimes subtle, but their impact can be profound.

Students' interpretations of setbacks and negative performance outcomes play a key role in determining whether their creativity will be supported or suppressed. Sometimes creative suppression is subtle and temporary. A teacher, for instance, inadvertently dismisses a student's idea. The student feels slighted, but the student is not dissuaded from sharing ideas at some later point in the lesson. Other times, creative suppression can be more profound. A student who has a creative aspiration to be a writer may give up on that dream as a result of receiving negative feedback on what she feels is her best work. This latter case of suppression has been called *creative mortification* (Beghetto, 2013, 2014).

Creative mortification refers to the loss of one's willingness to pursue a creative aspiration following a negative performance outcome (Beghetto, 2014). Of course not all students who receive negative feedback or experience negative performance outcomes will experience creative mortification. Some, in fact, may be motivated to continue to improve based on negative outcomes. Why might the same negative outcome extinguish the spark in one person and light a fire in another? Results from a recent study (Beghetto, 2014) shed some light on why this might be the case. There are a couple of key factors that seem to be at play. One is whether the person experiences shame as a result of the negative outcome. Shame is a strong and special type of emotion that can result in a person internalizing a failure (Lewis & Sullivan, 2005; Tracy & Robins, 2006). Another factor is whether the person feels improvement is possible. As prior research has consistently demonstrated (Dweck, 1999, 2006), a person who holds a fixed ability belief (i.e., believes that improvement is not possible) is less likely to pursue a goal in the face of challenges or setbacks. Taken together, the experience of shame and fixed ability beliefs seem to play a key role in determining whether a student will be mortified or motivated by negative performance outcomes (Beghetto, 2014).

Teachers can play a key role in helping increase the chances that students feel supported (rather than shamed) and willing to continue to improve (rather than give up). One way to think about the motivational messages sent by the learning environment is that what matters most is not what teachers intended by any particular classroom practice, policy, or procedure, but rather how students experience those features of the classroom environment. Teachers need to monitor actively how students are experiencing their classroom so they do not inadvertently undermine student motivation, learning, and creativity. The purpose of this chapter was to highlight some key insights from the research literature on motivation and provide concrete examples and suggestions that can help teachers establish a learning environment that supports (rather than inadvertently undermines) motivation, learning, and creativity.

A motivating learning environment serves as the bedrock for learning and creativity. Students need to feel supported in order to put forth creative effort and take reasonable intellectual risks in their learning. With a sound motivational foundation in place, teachers can make slight adjustments to their existing lessons—or even design new lessons—that effectively blend the Common Core with creativity. What are some features of a learning environment that simultaneously support learning and creativity?

Listed below are a few messages that a motivating environment sends to students (adapted from Beghetto, 2013, p. 143):

- You have time to think and work on tasks without needing to worry about constant evaluation and monitoring from your teachers or peers;
- You are encouraged to explore and integrate your interests and ideas into assignments and learning activities;
- You can learn as much if not more from making mistakes as you can from getting correct answers;
- The primary goal in this classroom is self-improvement and how you are doing now in comparison to how you have done before;
- You have freedom to generate messy ideas, take intellectual risks, and try new things that might result in mistakes; and
- The reason why you put forth effort is that you see the value in the task at hand, you are focused on improvement, and you are interested in and enjoy the task.

As a teacher you may recognize that you have been trying to include many of the above features in your classroom, but that you may need to focus on ensuring that these messages are more systematic and explicit, and are actually getting through to students. You may also recognize that there are some aspects of your classroom you need to adjust, some of which may come quite easily and others that may take time. Whether you view the ideas presented in this chapter as reaffirming of your views, inspirational, or aspirational, the key thesis is that approaching teaching creativity and the Common Core is an incremental effort—striving each day to improve, to try new things, to learn from mistakes, and to strive continually for the development of a learning environment in which you and your students are willing to share ideas, learn from one another, take intellectual risks, and express and develop your creative potential.

With a working understanding of how to establish a supportive learning environment, the next step is to understand how to combine creativity and the Common Core State Standards more systematically. Chapters 4 and 5 provide an overview of various insights, examples, and suggestions for infusing creativity and Common Core State Standards into ELA and Mathematics lessons.

CHAPTER 4

Practical Applications 1

Creative Lessons and Insights in English and Language Arts

Vignette 1: Meanings of Words in Various Contexts

In her 7th-grade Language Arts class Ms. Paton read Robert Frost's poem "The Road Not Taken" to her class after giving each student a copy of the poem so they could read along. Their assignment was to write poems of their own using only the words in "The Road Not Taken." A student's poem could be on any topic and didn't need to follow the form of the original poem (so it didn't need to rhyme and could be on any subject). After writing and sharing these poems with other students, the class discussed the original poem and tried to uncover its meaning. In particular, they focused on how the meaning of the words in the poem might differ from the meanings of the same words in other poems (such as the ones the students had written) and how we can ascertain the meanings of words in different contexts.

Common Core State Standards Addressed

➤ CCSS.ELA-Literacy.RL.7.4. Determine the meaning of words and phrases as they are used in a text, including figurative and connotative meanings; analyze the impact of rhymes and other repetitions of sounds (e.g., alliteration) on a specific verse or stanza of a poem or section of a story or drama.
➤ CCSS.ELA-Literacy.W.6.3d. Use precise words and phrases, relevant descriptive details, and sensory language to convey experiences and events.
➤ CCSS.ELA-Literacy.RL.3.4. Determine the meaning of words and phrases as they are used in a text, distinguishing literal from nonliteral language.

➤ CCSS.ELA-Literacy.RL.9-10.4. Determine the meaning of words and phrases as they are used in the text, including figurative and connotative meanings; analyze the cumulative impact of specific word choices on meaning and tone (e.g., how the language evokes a sense of time and place; how it sets a formal or informal tone).
➤ CCSS.ELA-Literacy.RL.5.4. Determine the meaning of words and phrases as they are used in a text, including figurative language such as metaphors and similes. (NGACPB & CCSSO, 2014b)

Analysis. Having students create the kinds of things they are being asked to analyze will both promote creativity and improve analytic skills. It will help students think about the meanings of words and how words change meaning based on context. It will provide an outlet for students' creativity, show that the teacher values the production of poetry by students, and give students the experience of writing a poem using an unusual set of constraints. In doing these things it will enhance both skill development and creative expression.

Summary. Vignette 1 illustrates how encouraging creativity in poetry can also promote skill in analyzing poetry (and perhaps vice versa). It could be used in connection with several of the English Language Arts Standards in different grades. The vignette comes from a 7th-grade classroom, but one can see how this activity might work with other Standards at other grade levels (a few of which are listed below).

Vignette 2: Writing Dialogue and Writing Creatively

Students in Ms. Robertson's English class had been learning how to use dialogue in stories. They had studied how authors utilized dialogue in the assigned stories; Ms. Robertson next asked the class to write stories of their own using dialogue that had the same strengths as the material they had studied. She provided a rubric with markers such as "the dialogue is believable and meaningful," "different kinds of dialogue constructions are used," "the dialogue helps reveal character," "the dialogue contributes to the action in the story," "the dialogue helps develop conflicts in the story," and "the dialogue is punctuated appropriately." She told students that these are the only things she would be attending to when evaluating and grading their stories so they should focus very much on how they used dialogue in their stories, as delineated by the rubric she gave them.

Two weeks later, in an unrelated activity, Ms. Robertson asked her students to write another story, but this time she told them that there would be no evaluation or grading. If students wrote stories that were in any way imaginative they would automatically get an A, but any student who failed to do the assignment at all would get an F. There would be no other grades. She encouraged students to have fun with their stories, to take chances, to try to write something really interesting, to use any techniques they had learned in their reading and writing to make it the most interesting and creative story possible, and to write stories that they and their classmates might enjoy reading—but most of all, to write stories that they themselves found interesting. Students were told they would have the option of sharing their stories with others, but this would not be a requirement. When Ms. Robertson read the stories that were turned in she kept her word—she gave no grades other than A (for any story that showed even minimal effort) and F (for students who failed to turn in a story). Her comments on students' papers were supportive but not evaluative (e.g., "Interesting story!" "It looks like you had a good time writing this!" "I really enjoyed reading your story!").

Common Core State Standards Addressed

➤ CCSS.ELA-Literacy.W.9-10.3b. Use narrative techniques, such as dialogue, pacing, description, reflection, and multiple plot lines, to develop experiences, events, and/or characters.

➤ CCSS.ELA-Literacy.W.11-12.3b. Use narrative techniques, such as dialogue, pacing, description, reflection, and multiple plot lines, to develop experiences, events, and/or characters. (NGACPB & CCSSO, 2014b)

Analysis. One way that teaching for skill-building and teaching for creativity conflict with each other—it's a partial conflict, but a conflict that can be hard to avoid in classrooms—involves extrinsic constraints such as evaluation. As we have discussed, there is a large body of research that shows that students tend to be less creative when they expect that their work will be evaluated (Amabile, 1996; Baer, 1997, 1998; Hennessey & Zbikowski, 1993). In fact, there is research that has set up situations very much like what students were asked to do in these two assignments. When students anticipate that their work will be evaluated they tend to write less creative stories than when they believe that their work will not be evaluated (Amabile, 1979; Amabile, Goldfarb, & Brackfield, 1990). Evaluation that focuses on the story itself (e.g., "Excellent use of dialogue to help the reader understand this character's inner motivations" or "The dialogue here doesn't seem to add much to the story") is less harmful than evaluation that focuses on the writer (e.g., "The way you used dialogue here shows you have real talent for writing!"), but either kind of evaluation tends to depress creativity (and bear in mind that positive feedback, while more pleasant both to give and to receive, focuses students' attention on evaluation just as much as negative feedback and leads in the same way to an increase in extrinsic motivation and a decrease in intrinsic motivation). As stated in Chapter 3, there are two general findings from research about extrinsic and intrinsic motivation:

- Intrinsic motivation—doing something because one finds it interesting, enjoyable, or meaningful, or because one wants to develop a skill or talent—tends to increase creativity; and extrinsic motivation—doing something to earn a reward or in anticipation of evaluation by others—can decrease creativity.
- Extrinsic motivation can drive out intrinsic motivation. This is sometimes called the "hidden cost of reward." When rewards are used as bribes to get students to do things those students already like to do (e.g., rewarding students who already like to read for reading books), the students' level of intrinsic motivation decreases. They may do more of the activity (e.g., read more books) when the reward (bribe) is operative, but they are very likely to read less than before once the reward is no longer available (Amabile, Hennessey, & Grossman, 1986). Extrinsic constraints like rewards and evaluations can have what look like positive short-term effects but that then exact considerable long-term damage. When bribes (offered as rewards for compliance) are offered for doing activities that students already enjoy doing, they can turn what was fun into work and make it less likely that students will want to do those things once the rewards stop coming.

So evaluations can have a negative impact on students' creativity, at least in the short term. But at the same time, much research (and common sense) shows that to develop skills, students need feedback (aka evaluation). So in the short term, emphasizing evaluation (as in Ms. Robertson's first story assignment) is likely to build skills, but also to depress creativity. What's a teacher who cares about both skill development and creativity to do?

Ms. Robertson has an excellent answer—do both, but at different times. Sometimes (much of the time), teachers need to have students working on skill development; this is a key component of CCSS. However, skill development often requires evaluation. Teachers need to understand that this focus is necessary but that it will also likely result in less creative performance on the task that's under evaluation. In Ms. Robertson's first assignment, students would emphasize getting it right. They are asked (perhaps a bit too self-consciously) to use dialogue in the ways they have studied and which are listed on the rubric, and are asked to expend much effort on specific tasks, such as correct punctuation and dialogue construction. Taking risks, pushing boundaries, or emphasizing creativity are not things this activity is likely to foster, and it may also dampen some students' intrinsic motivation for writing.

However, in her second writing assignment 2 weeks later Ms. Robertson removed the evaluation constraints (or at least got them down to a bare minimum). This modification should allow intrinsic motivation to surface. It's hard to *create* intrinsic motivation; often the best we can do is get out of its way by downplaying extrinsic constraints. In this second activity Ms. Robertson showed that she appreciates writing as an activity that has value in and of itself. She encouraged creativity and experimentation and she gave students room to take risks. Might some students abuse this kind of freedom from evaluation? Of course they might—and some students will test limits and do the minimum amount of work. But other students will make good use of such an opportunity, which will nurture both their creativity and their interest in writing. Meanwhile, the students who did not take advantage of this opportunity will not be harmed in any way. They will just have wasted some time and thrown away an opportunity to do something interesting (and, it's important to remember, they will still have to do the other types of writing assignments that do get evaluated), whereas the students who like writing can try something interesting and get a chance to enjoy creative writing.

The same ideas should guide writing activities in elementary classrooms. Sometimes student writing should be evaluated, based on explicit criteria as set forth in rubrics. Other times, student writing is for fun and should be subject to only the most minimal evaluation. Students need to be told in advance, of course, which rules apply. If it isn't made very clear (and if teachers don't honor the rules they have announced), students will simply assume that there will be evaluation, given that it is a school assignment. There is a fringe benefit for teachers, as well. On these no-evaluation assignments all they need to do is read and enjoy the students' stories, not grade them!

The first writing activity (with a rubric and an evaluation) will help students develop their skills as writers. Even though it may suppress their creativity on that assignment, it will also help them develop some of the writing tools they will need to become better creative writers. So a lesson focusing on skill development can have both a negative (short-term) and a positive (long-term) impact on student creativity.

The second writing activity (without the evaluation) can help remedy these negative short-term effects. Providing time for the type of writing Ms. Robertson established with her second writing assignment is important. If everything a student writes is evaluated, his or her intrinsic interest in writing will slowly be driven out. We don't want to help students develop the skills they need to be creative writers at the cost of killing all interest in creative writing. We need to do both skill instruction and development *and* creativity nurturance and enhancement. But sometimes we need to do those things at different times and with different assignments.

Summary. The above vignette is actually two, because there are two seemingly similar assignments that the teacher sets up in two very different ways, one focused on skill development and the other on creative expression. These two vignettes highlight one way in which teaching for the Common Core State Standards and teaching for creativity conflict, and they demonstrate how to provide lessons that accommodate both. The Standard being addressed is the same in the listing for both Grades 9–10 and Grades 11–12 and could be used in any high school English class (with adjustments to fit the students' current knowledge of how to use dialogue in narrative writing). The basic idea for the lessons described could also be modified for teaching other parts of this Standard, such as pacing, description, reflection, and use of multiple plot lines. The central idea (about how to use extrinsic constraints to promote skill development and intrinsic motivation to promote creativity) is equally relevant in classrooms at all levels from K through 12.

Vignette 3: Divergent Thinking During Character Brainstorming and Comparison

Ms. Ellis taped three large sheets of newsprint to the board in her 5th-grade classroom and wrote "Harry" atop one, "Hermione" on another, and "Hagrid" on the third. "Today we're going to think about three of the characters we've been reading about and look at ways they're alike and ways they're different."

"What about Ron?" asked a student at a table in the back.

"Ron's an important character," Ms. Ellis said, "and when you do your own comparisons you can use Ron if you'd like. Or Professor Dumbledore, or Draco Malfoy, or anyone else in the book. But for what we're doing right now, just these three. What I'd like to do is think about things we know about each of these three characters. We're going to use the brainstorming rules we've used before," she said, pointing to a chart on the wall that read:

Brainstorming Rules
Defer judgment.
Avoid ownership of ideas.
Feel free to "hitchhike" on other ideas.
Wild ideas are encouraged.
(adapted from Baer & Kaufman, 2012)

"So remember, every idea is a good idea. Later we'll go back and decide which ideas we want to use. Now, who can tell me something about Hermione?" Several hands shot up. "Jasmine?"

"She's smart," Jasmine called out gleefully.

Ms. Ellis wrote "smart" on the far left side of the paper. "Jacob?"

"Her parents are muggles," he said, giggling a little.

Ms. Ellis wrote "muggle parents" below "smart."

After several more things were added to the list, there were no more hands. "Remember, every idea's a good idea. What else do we know, or maybe think we know, about Hermione?"

A girl raised her hand tentatively. "I think maybe she's a little shy."

Ms. Ellis wrote "shy."

Another girl asked, "I think she might be sad sometimes?"

Ms. Ellis wrote "sad."

When the class agreed they had described Hermione pretty well, Ms. Ellis explained that now they would discuss the ideas, so evaluation was okay—they were no longer brainstorming or following brainstorming rules. "Let's see how these ideas work and what evidence we can provide for them. We said that maybe Hermione is smart. How do we know she's smart?"

"She likes to read, and whenever she has a problem she goes to the library to find answers." "The teachers think she's smart." "She always knows the answers."

Ms. Ellis wrote "likes to read, uses library, knows answers, teachers say so" next to "smart."

"So we're pretty sure she's smart because we have lots of evidence for that. Now, how do we know her parents are muggles?"

"The book says so. She says so."

Ms. Ellis wrote, "She told us." "We didn't really need to figure out that she was a muggle, did we? The book told us this directly. Hmmm. Did the book tell us she's smart? Or did we have to figure that out?" The class quickly agreed that the book told readers that her parents were muggles, and Ms. Ellis helped them see how the ways we know Hermione is smart are different; we have to figure out that she's smart based on things she does and stories from the book.

Ms. Ellis went through the list, having students explain how they know the various things on the list describe Hermione. "Sad" was on the list, but most of the students said that they don't think she's sad, and no one could think of any time in the book she seemed sad. After this discussion, the class decided Hermione isn't really sad and Ms. Ellis drew a thin line through it. "If we can't find any evidence, we can't know that it's true, can we? But I'm just lightly scratching this out—it's still there, so if we do discover evidence for it later on we can put it back—but for now we won't include it in our description of Hermione."

When she got to "shy" no one was quite sure why they thought she was shy, but several students said they still thought this described her. Ms. Ellis suggested they look back through the book to see if they could find evidence, which after a few minutes they did. Some evidence was produced, but not everyone was convinced that "shy" really applies to Hermione.

"We don't have to agree on this," Ms. Ellis said, "but if you think she's shy then perhaps you need to go back through the book to find more evidence. And if you think she's not shy, the same thing applies—you need to go back through the book to find times when she didn't act shyly." Finally, Ms. Ellis asked the class to think about which of the characteristics they had listed were the most important. She asked each student to make her or his own list of Hermione's three most important characteristics from the list. After they did that, she had students compare their lists at their tables.

"Remember, we don't all have to agree," Ms. Ellis said.

The class followed the same process for Harry and Hagrid. Forty-five minutes later they had newsprint papers filled with characteristics of the three characters. Each characteristic brainstormed by the class included supporting evidence. Each student had an individual list of the three most important characteristics for all three characters.

"Have we described these characters well? I think we have. You know how to do this now. So next I want you to pick out one more character from the book and, on your own, brainstorm a list of things we know, or think we know, about that character. Try to come up with as many things as you can say about the character you pick and leave a few lines open between each thing you write."

After doing this, Ms. Ellis asked the students to think of evidence for each thing they wrote down. "If you decide you can't really find evidence, then it's okay to drop something from your list."

The next day, Ms. Ellis had summarized what was on the newsprint and listed it on three handouts, which she passed out to the students. She asked the class to get out the lists they had made. "What I'd like you to do is think about which of these three characters is the most like the character you chose for your personal list, and which character is least like the one chose. Take a few minutes to think about that. It's a good idea to compare the different lists to see if that gives you any ideas. If you think of something you want to add to any of the lists, that's fine." She walked around the class as they worked, looking at students' papers and asking them questions about their lists.

"Okay, here's the last thing, class. I want you to write two short essays. One should be about how your character and one of the three characters we did together are alike, and the other essay should be about how your character and one of the three are different. Make sure to include evidence. How do you know that the character is shy or proud or loud or whatever it is you think makes them similar to, or very unlike, the other character?"

Common Core State Standards Addressed

➤ CCSS.ELA-Literacy.RL.5.3. Compare and contrast two or more characters, settings, or events in a story or drama, drawing on specific details in the text (e.g., how characters interact). (NGACPB & CCSSO, 2014b).

Analysis. This vignette makes use of divergent thinking at several places. Is it central to the activity? Perhaps not. Someone could make the argument that some creative thinking is required for the essentially analytical process of the compare-and-contrast assignment, but we think it would still be the case that creativity isn't a major theme in this lesson. But bear in mind that although promoting creativity in classrooms is important, it probably shouldn't be front and center in every lesson. There are times when creativity simply needs to play a supporting role, as it does here. And divergent thinking (whether produced via brainstorming rules or other instructions, such as, "Think of many, varied, and unusual ideas about X") can play a supporting role in *many* lessons at all grade levels in similar ways. We often want students to consider a range of possibilities before making a decision or a judgment; what better way than to have students generate a number of possible choices first? They not only improve their skills in the activity that is the focus of the lesson (in this vignette, doing a compare/contrast analysis) but they also get a chance to exercise and strengthen their divergent-thinking muscles, which are important components of creativity.

Summary. This is a rather detailed vignette that shows how divergent thinking (during brainstorming) can be a part of many different kinds of lessons and at multiple places in the lesson. Note that the brainstorming activity is probably interesting to students, yet it is not at all silly; it is not another variant on "unusual uses of a brick." In addition, the activity is used as a way to generate ideas for further exploration, so it has a purpose. The goal is not to teach brainstorming—the teacher using this activity knows that her students have learned the basic concepts of brainstorming and have practiced with the technique previously. Therefore, a basic knowledge of brainstorming is a prerequisite for this lesson.

Vignette 4: Distinguishing Among Fact, Opinion, and Reasoned Judgment

---

Mr. Tandy's 8th-grade social studies class had been studying the newspaper, using a lesson plan from the *New York Times* (Brown & Schulten, 2013). Believing his students had a strong understanding of how to distinguish among fact, opinion, and reasoned judgment, Mr. Tandy gave this assignment:

> Find a news story (not an opinion piece) in the *New York Times* about which different people might have different opinions. The story needn't be current; students are welcome to surf through older editions of the newspaper or use the online search function to find stories about some topic the student finds interesting or simply thinks it might be interesting to write about. Print out the story so you have a copy to work with and to turn in with your assignment. Your job is to write two different editorials by two people who would come to the story with very different sets of beliefs, opinions, and/or biases.

After the students had written and turned in their editorials, Mr. Tandy made a copy of each of the editorials and randomly distributed the editorials (but not the news stories) to the class (so each student received two editorials about different topics that he or she did not write). The students' task then was to identify which parts of the editorials were factual, which parts were opinion, and which parts were reasoned judgment.

Common Core State Standards Addressed

➤ CCSS.ELA-Literacy.RH.6-8.8. Distinguish among fact, opinion, and reasoned judgment in a text. (NGACPB & CCSSO, 2014b)

Analysis. Separating fact, opinion, and reasoned judgment is an important skill, but not one that always generates a great deal of student interest. This lesson combines learning how to make such distinctions with a creative writing activity (writing the editorials). Students were asked both to create opinions and reasoned judgments and combine them with the facts of a news article. They were then asked to disentangle these elements in other students' editorials, giving them a chance to use these skills in connection with a different content.

This activity could be adapted to meet these additional high school Literacy in History/Social Studies Standards:

➤ CCSS.ELA-Literacy.RH.9-10.6. Compare the point of view of two or more authors for how they treat the same or similar topics, including which details they include and emphasize in their respective accounts.

➤ CCSS.ELA-Literacy.RH.11-12.6. Evaluate authors' differing points of view on the same historical event or issue by assessing the authors' claims, reasoning, and evidence. (NGACPB & CCSSO, 2014b)

This activity could also be adapted to focus on science reporting to work toward these middle school and high school Literacy in Science Standards:

> ➤ CCSS.ELA-Literacy.RST.6-8.8. Distinguish among facts, reasoned judgment based on research findings, and speculation in a text.
> ➤ CCSS.ELA-Literacy.RST.9-10.8. Assess the extent to which the reasoning and evidence in a text support the author's claim or a recommendation for solving a scientific or technical problem.
> ➤ CCSS.ELA-Literacy.RST.11-12.8. Evaluate the hypotheses, data, analysis, and conclusions in a science or technical text, verifying the data when possible and corroborating or challenging conclusions with other sources of information. (NGACPB & CCSSO, 2014b)

Summary. This is a vignette that could be used to meet an important Literacy in History/Social Studies Standard about separating fact, opinion, and reasoned judgment. The vignette describes a middle school social studies activity but could easily be adapted for high school history and middle school or high school science (the relevant Standards for these adaptations are noted above).

Vignette 5: Verb Tense and Student Storytelling

The students in Ms. Daniels's 5th-grade class had been studying verb tense. They seemed to understand the basic concepts, so she asked her students to describe an event the way someone might describe an event in the past, by using the past tense. She started the activity by giving them two examples—one from sports and another from an imagined event in history ("The day the first car drove into town")—to give students an idea of what she expected. She then asked students to brainstorm the kinds of events one might describe in the past tense. She listed those ideas on the Smartboard.

The students were then encouraged to write interesting accounts of an event (whether one from the list on the Smartboard or one from their imagination). They could describe any kind of event from the recent or far distant past. The one constraint was that the stories should be events that could possibly have happened, even though these would be made-up stories about made-up events. So, for example, students were not supposed to write about an alien invasion.

Ms. Daniels was pleased that the class seemed to do this successfully. The next day she handed back those papers and gave a new assignment: Describe the same event again, but this time in the present tense as an event that is happening now. Their stories should sound more like a play-by-play description of the event, using the present tense appropriately. She modeled this herself, using a modified version of "Casey at the Bat." Her aim was to show how sometimes simply changing the tense of the verb wasn't enough or required making tough decisions about how to say something. For example, should "Everyone watched him as he stepped up to the plate" become "Everyone watches him as he steps up to the plate" or "Everyone is watching him as he steps up to the plate" or something else? And what should one do with the closing sentence, "Mighty Casey has struck out?" Might it sometimes make sense, even in a play-by-play, present-tense account of an event, to use a past tense ("Mighty Casey struck out.")? Or should one stick to the present tense ("Mighty Casey strikes out.")? The class helped her make the change from past to present tense for her story about Casey—not always agreeing on what would be the best way, so Ms. Daniels recorded all the possibilities that were deemed to be acceptable choices—and then did the same for their own stories (i.e., they rewrote them to be in the present tense).

Common Core State Standards Addressed

➤ CCSS.ELA-Literacy.L.5.1c. Use verb tense to convey various times, sequences, states, and conditions. (NGACPB & CCSSO, 2014b)

Analysis. This lesson is about an important literacy standard (verb tense), and the papers that students turn in should be evaluated according to the correctness of verb tense. However, this assignment also gives students a chance to write their own stories. Regardless of the level of creativity in their story, they are actively engaged in a creative activity. In addition, the lesson gives students a chance to use divergent thinking (produced via brainstorming) to create a list of many possible ideas for stories (see Vignette 3 for a discussion of the many ways to practice divergent thinking while also developing skills outlined in the Standards).

Issues about evaluation and its impact on creativity (as discussed in Vignette 2) also arise here. At this grade level and with the fairly minimal constraints that Ms. Daniels put on the first story, it seems unlikely that students' intrinsic motivation for writing stories would be much dampened. There was a focus on getting the tense correct, but otherwise students were reasonably free to let their imaginations take them to interesting places. The brainstorming activity should have helped induce an atmosphere of (almost) "anything goes" regarding the topic of the imagined events. But one would hope that Ms. Daniels would occasionally use the same technique as Ms. Robertson in Vignette 2 and offer her students even more freedom from evaluation in some of their writing activities, thereby encouraging creativity and nurturing students' intrinsic motivation for writing imaginative stories.

Summary. This is a vignette about telling a story with a focus on the use of verb tense. It involves making up one's own story and then telling it using a different tense. This vignette illustrates how the simple combination of an academic goal (i.e., verb tense) and students' unique ideas (e.g., making up their own story) can result in a creative lesson.

HOW TO TEACH FOR CREATIVITY WHILE TEACHING THE ENGLISH LANGUAGE ARTS (ELA) COMMON CORE

We want to be honest: There are ways in which teaching for creativity and teaching to help students acquire the skills and knowledge outlined in the ELA Common Core sometimes conflict. The two do not always push teachers in the same directions, and this tension can sometimes lead to serious challenges for teachers who care about teaching for creativity.

But there are as many ways (if not more) in which the two goals *do* cooperate. There are ways in which teaching for creativity supports learning the skills and knowledge of the ELA Common Core and ways in which teaching to the ELA Common Core can also nurture students' creativity. Some of those synergies are obvious and others less so. Let's start with what is probably the most obvious of these synergies: To be creative readers, thinkers, and writers, students need to acquire fundamental literacy skills.

Here are the Common Core College and Career Readiness Anchor Standards for Reading:

College and Career Readiness Anchor Standards for Reading

Key Ideas and Details

1. Read closely to determine what the text says explicitly and to make logical inferences from it; cite specific textual evidence when writing or speaking to support conclusions drawn from the text.
2. Determine central ideas or themes of a text and analyze their development; summarize the key supporting details and ideas.
3. Analyze how and why individuals, events, and ideas develop and interact over the course of a text.

Craft and Structure

4. Interpret words and phrases as they are used in a text, including determining technical, connotative, and figurative meanings, and analyze how specific word choices shape meaning or tone.

5. Analyze the structure of texts, including how specific sentences, paragraphs, and larger portions of the text (e.g., a section, chapter, scene, or stanza) relate to one another and the whole.
6. Assess how point of view or purpose shapes the content and style of a text.

Integration of Knowledge and Ideas

7. Integrate and evaluate content presented in diverse media and formats, including visually and quantitatively, as well as in words.
8. Delineate and evaluate the argument and specific claims in a text, including the validity of the reasoning as well as the relevance and sufficiency of the evidence.
9. Analyze how two or more texts address similar themes or topics in order to build knowledge or to compare the approaches the authors take.

Range of Reading and Level of Text Complexity

10. Read and comprehend complex literary and informational texts independently and proficiently. (NGACPB & CCSSO, 2014b)

Is there anything in that list that isn't fundamental to creativity? Here is a second list, this one from the *College and Career Readiness Anchor Standards for Writing*:

College and Career Readiness Anchor Standards for Writing

Text Types and Purposes

1. Write arguments to support claims in an analysis of substantive topics or texts, using valid reasoning and relevant and sufficient evidence.
2. Write informative/explanatory texts to examine and convey complex ideas and information clearly and accurately through the effective selection, organization, and analysis of content.
3. Write narratives to develop real or imagined experiences or events using effective technique, well-chosen details, and well-structured event sequences.

Production and Distribution of Writing

4. Produce clear and coherent writing in which the development, organization, and style are appropriate to task, purpose, and audience.

5. Develop and strengthen writing as needed by planning, revising, editing, rewriting, or trying a new approach.
6. Use technology, including the Internet, to produce and publish writing and to interact and collaborate with others.

Research to Build and Present Knowledge

7. Conduct short as well as more sustained research projects based on focused questions, demonstrating understanding of the subject under investigation.
8. Gather relevant information from multiple print and digital sources, assess the credibility and accuracy of each source, and integrate the information while avoiding plagiarism.
9. Draw evidence from literary or informational texts to support analysis, reflection, and research.

Range of Writing

10. Write routinely over extended time frames (time for research, reflection, and revision) and shorter time frames (a single sitting or a day or two) for a range of tasks, purposes, and audiences. (NGACPB & CCSSO, 2014b)

Then there are the *College and Career Readiness Anchor Standards for Speaking and Listening*:

College and Career Readiness Anchor Standards for Speaking and Listening

Comprehension and Collaboration

1. Prepare for and participate effectively in a range of conversations and collaborations with diverse partners, building on others' ideas and expressing their own clearly and persuasively.
2. Integrate and evaluate information presented in diverse media and formats, including visually, quantitatively, and orally.
3. Evaluate a speaker's point of view, reasoning, and use of evidence and rhetoric.

Presentation of Knowledge and Ideas

4. Present information, findings, and supporting evidence such that listeners can follow the line of reasoning and the organization, development, and style are appropriate to task, purpose, and audience.

5. Make strategic use of digital media and visual displays of data to express information and enhance understanding of presentations.
6. Adapt speech to a variety of contexts and communicative tasks, demonstrating command of formal English when indicated or appropriate. (NGACPB & CCSSO, 2014b)

And finally, here are the *College and Career Readiness Anchor Standards for Language*, which may seem the most conformity-inducing of the four sets of ELA Anchor Standards:

College and Career Readiness Anchor Standards for Language

Conventions of Standard English

1. Demonstrate command of the conventions of standard English grammar and usage when writing or speaking.
2. Demonstrate command of the conventions of standard English capitalization, punctuation, and spelling when writing.

Knowledge of Language

3. Apply knowledge of language to understand how language functions in different contexts, to make effective choices for meaning or style, and to comprehend more fully when reading or listening.

Vocabulary Acquisition and Use

4. Determine or clarify the meaning of unknown and multiple-meaning words and phrases by using context clues, analyzing meaningful word parts, and consulting general and specialized reference materials, as appropriate.
5. Demonstrate understanding of figurative language, word relationships, and nuances in word meanings.
6. Acquire and use accurately a range of general academic and domain-specific words and phrases sufficient for reading, writing, speaking, and listening at the college and career readiness level; demonstrate independence in gathering vocabulary knowledge when considering a word or phrase [to be] important to comprehension or expression. (NGACPB & CCSSO, 2014b)

The Common Core ELA's College and Career Readiness Anchor Standards—even the ones about the conventions of grammar, punctuation, and spelling—are all representative of skills that are necessary (albeit not sufficient) requirements for many kinds of English Language Arts creativity. There is no obvious conflict in having these standards as goals; these are skills and knowledge that even those of us who are most passionately devoted to nurturing student creativity hope our students will develop and, therefore, things we want to teach our students. These skills will help students be more creative in the future—*if*, in the process of teaching them these skills, we don't kill off their creativity, undermine their intrinsic interest in reading and writing, or force underground their joy in pushing boundaries and trying new things.

So it's important that, while teaching the many skills embodied in the Common Core, we do not forget one of the key reasons that they are learning these skills—so they can be more creative! We must also remember, even when we are teaching the Common Core, that we still need to nurture creativity whenever we can, encourage students' intrinsic motivation to read and to write, and make learning as interesting and engaging as possible. Fortunately, the Common Core still allows us to do all those things. We needn't adopt the kinds of mind-numbing drills and lifeless activities that take all the fun out of learning.

Let's look again at Vignette 1, which is a model for many other activities teachers can use at almost all levels when teaching the ELA Common Core. The teacher in Vignette 1 asked students to create a poem of their own using only the words from the poem they were studying (Robert Frost's "The Road Not Taken"). The two seemingly unrelated goals were both to write a poem and explore how words have different meanings in different contexts. As we indicated in the introduction to that vignette, the same activity could be used (with appropriate modifications) to meet similar Standards at many different grade levels. Similarly, the idea of having students produce the kinds of writing the Standards ask them to analyze (under several different Standards) can be reached, in part, by having students do some creative writing at the same time that they are learning the skills embodied in the Standard. Consider the first three *College and Career Readiness Anchor Standards for Reading*:

1. Read closely to determine what the text says explicitly and to make logical inferences from it; cite specific textual evidence when writing or speaking to support conclusions drawn from the text.
2. Determine central ideas or themes of a text and analyze their development; summarize the key supporting details and ideas.
3. Analyze how and why individuals, events, and ideas develop and interact over the course of a text. (NGACPB & CCSSO, 2014b)

Teachers could have students do an activity in which they read an essay and then write an essay of their own in which they "unpack" the arguments in the assigned paper, as if they were explaining it to someone who didn't understand the key ideas, conclusions, and evidence. This task would require students to determine what the text says and what it implies. They would need to evaluate what evidence the text uses to make its claims, and what the key ideas are and how they have been developed. After some work learning how to do these things, students could then use the skills in their own essays as they explain the ideas and arguments in the original paper. Students might imagine a less perceptive reader who might not "get" the author's intended meaning and they could use their own words to explain the original paper to such a reader.

One could do something similar with a standard that falls under the College and Career Readiness Anchor Standards for Reading 6—"assess how point of view or purpose shapes the content and style of a text"—by rewriting the text from a different point of view or with a different purpose. Or consider the College and Career Readiness Anchor Standards for Language 5: "Demonstrate understanding of figurative language, word relationships, and nuances in word meanings." What better way to learn how to understand figurative language than to use it in one's own writing? Of course, almost all of the College and Career Readiness Anchor Standards for Writing lend themselves to this kind of activity.

It is important to bear in mind in designing activities of this kind that creative writing is not limited to fiction, or even to creative nonfiction. Writing an interesting essay requires creativity, as does writing an interesting description of a scene or event (even an interesting description of, say, a sporting event). Teachers can give students a chance to do some creative writing while also learning or practicing many of the ELA Common Core State Standards.

Vignette 2 also offers a model that could be used in other ways, for different Standards and at different grade levels. As we have discussed earlier, Amabile (1996) conducted a series of studies which found that when students anticipate evaluation of their work they tend to do less creative work. Many of her studies involved writing activities (either poems or short stories). When students were told that their work would be evaluated, or if they simply assumed it would be evaluated because past assignments had been evaluated, this extrinsic constraint (anticipated evaluation) tended to drive out intrinsic motivation, the result being less creative poems and stories. This was true at all grade levels, and later research has suggested that this is actually more true for girls than for boys (Baer, 1997, 1998). Creativity tends to decrease, particularly in girls, when they know (or assume) that their work will be evaluated.

However, in order to help students develop English Language Arts skills, teachers need to provide feedback, and feedback is just a gentle way of saying evaluation. Anticipated evaluation isn't limited to grading. Even in studies where students received only positive feedback and suggestions on an initial story—no grades or criticism of their writing, just comments on what was good or what worked in their stories—when students did a second activity of the same kind they were less creative than students who had not received any feedback at all on their first effort (Amabile, 1996).

As we have said, incompatibilities can arise between teaching the Common Core and teaching to promote creativity. Sometimes teachers need to do things that they know will diminish creativity, at least in the short term and for the particular task at hand, in order to promote skill development. This is a situation in which teaching for creativity and teaching the Common Core seem to be in conflict—although, to reinforce a recurrent theme of this book, the conflict is only partial. Even though creativity may be lessened in the short term, the skills thus developed should contribute to more accomplished creative performance down the road.

The danger is that if *every* writing assignment results in evaluation, the negative impact on creativity and intrinsic motivation may be more than just short term. Students once interested in writing may lose that interest and give it up. What was fun can all too easily be turned into work. Sadly, this happens all the time in schools. Most primary-grade students who have learned how to read say they like reading, but if you ask students how much they enjoy reading in every grade, those numbers show a steady decline as students move through the grades. Play has become work and enjoyment has become tedium. It's not because the options that are available to young children when they read are more interesting than the options for older readers. It's that reading itself has become all work and no play. The same thing can, and sadly often does, happen with writing.

To help students maintain their interest in writing while also teaching them writing skills, we need to ask them to write under different conditions. Sometimes there will be rubrics for evaluating their work, based on whatever Standards or objectives a teacher has for the lesson. But other times, students simply need the opportunity to write and to have their writing valued but not evaluated. These types of assignments can free them to take chances, to push boundaries, to try things out—in short, to be creative. If some students abuse these opportunities (and some will), as we noted in discussing Vignette 2, that's okay. Most of their writing assignments will be graded. If they choose to squander the opportunities they are given to write without the fear of evaluation by seeing how little they can write and still get away with it, then no great harm will be done. The students who do enjoy writing will have their intrinsic motivation for writing (and their creativity) enhanced by such free, ungraded writing activities.

Vignette 3 is about the use of brainstorming (or other techniques for producing divergent thinking). Divergent thinking is an important part of creativity. In fact, it's so important that some teachers have acted as if divergent thinking is the same thing as creativity, which it is not. Divergent thinking is about coming up with many unusual ideas or responses to an open-ended prompt, but creativity has the additional requirement of being in some way useful or workable. A creative solution must fit the situation or solve the problem. Simply being original is not enough. But off-the-wall ideas can contribute to creativity, and that's where divergent thinking helps. If there is a large pool of possible ideas to choose from, then the odds are better that some of the ideas will be usable in real life.

So divergent thinking is one part of the creative process, and brainstorming (or similar techniques) produces divergent thinking. In many situations students are better off if they brainstorm possible ideas before choosing an idea, as exemplified in Vignette 3. It may be as simple as brainstorming possible events before predicting what might happen next (such as in a story, in an historical account, or in a science experiment); this scenario may only take a few minutes of brainstorming. For example, consider College and Career Readiness Anchor Standards for Writing Standard 1: "Write arguments to support claims in an analysis of substantive topics or texts, using valid reasoning and relevant and sufficient evidence" (NGACPB & CCSSO, 2014b). It will almost always be helpful to do some brainstorming (or brainwriting, as it is often called when one does it alone) to produce a list of *possible* arguments before writing such an essay.

Brainstorming can also have some uses that may not lead to a creative product or idea. In introducing a new topic, whether it is gerunds, Abraham Lincoln, a story about frogs, or the Apollo moon missions, it can be helpful to ask students to brainstorm what they know about the topic at the outset, before they begin to study it. When one does this, it is important to stick to the rules of brainstorming. If one student says "Abraham Lincoln was the first president" and another student tries to correct this, the teacher should remind the class that there is no judging of ideas during brainstorming—that comes later. But *after* brainstorming the teacher can go through the list and note misunderstandings or factual mistakes. This type of short brainstorming activity can activate students' background knowledge and will give the teacher a chance to find out what students already know. It will also allow teachers to clarify and correct misconceptions. The fact that it's also brainstorming practice is almost incidental to its use in such situations, but it will, nonetheless, help strengthen students' divergent thinking muscles.

In Vignette 4 the teacher had students write two editorials from two very different viewpoints about an actual news story (one that was not an editorial). In the analysis of Vignette 4, we discussed several other Literacy in History and Literacy in Science Standards that the activity would fit (with modifications, of course). The key in this kind of activity is (as in Vignette 1) to have students do something—create something—and in doing so learn better how that process works, which gets at the Common Core Standard being addressed. This activity could also be turned around by having students read two contrasting editorials that might appear as a point-counterpoint, and then write a news story based on those editorials that tries to drain them of any special perspectives—a news story that offers a balance of fact and reasoned judgment, but no opinion. Students might be asked to do this assignment using nothing more than the two contrasting editorials by figuring out what is fact, what is opinion, and what is reasoned judgment in those editorials to correspond with *CCSS.ELA-Literacy.RH.6-8.8*, "Distinguish among fact, opinion, and reasoned judgment in a text." Conversely, they might be asked to gather more information about the topic from different sources to produce a balanced perspective, which is consistent with *CCSS.ELA-Literacy.SL.9-10.3*, "Evaluate a speaker's point of view, reasoning, and use of evidence and rhetoric, identifying any fallacious reasoning or exaggerated or distorted evidence"; or *CCSS.ELA-Literacy.SL.9-10.2*, "Integrate multiple sources of information presented in diverse media or formats (e.g., visually, quantitatively, orally), evaluating the credibility and accuracy of each source" (NGACPB & CCSSO, 2014b).

In Vignette 5, students were asked to describe an event in a different tense. In the analysis of Vignette 5, we discussed how the issues raised by Vignette 2 (the impact of evaluation on intrinsic motivation and creativity) arise, and we want to stress the point that there may be multiple creativity-relevant issues at work in any lesson. The Standards that fall under the *College and Career Readiness Anchor Standards for Language* may be some of the most rule bound and arbitrary convention following of all the standards—for example, "Demonstrate command of the conventions of standard English grammar and usage when writing or speaking" and "Demonstrate command of the conventions of standard English capitalization, punctuation, and spelling when writing" (NGACPB & CCSSO, 2014b)—but they still leave room for creative writing activities that will both promote creativity and help students learn the required skills. One can focus on a particular skill—for example, CCSS. ELA-Literacy.L.4.2a ("Use correct capitalization"), CCSS.ELA-Literacy.L.7.1c ("Place phrases and clauses within a sentence, recognizing and correcting misplaced and dangling modifiers"), or CCSS.ELA-Literacy.L.9-10.1a ("Use parallel structure") (NGACPB & CCSSO, 2014b)—and tell students they must demonstrate in their writing assignment that they understand how to use these conventions by using them correctly. However, the rest of the story is totally up to them, and nothing beyond the correct usage of the specific rule will be graded or evaluated by the teacher in any way; it will only be read and enjoyed.

The preceding vignettes and our discussion of them are just starting points for the vast creativity of teachers, who can find many more ways to link teaching for creativity and teaching the ELA Common Core State Standards. As we have repeatedly stated, the CCSS and creativity may sometimes seem to be at odds (as in the conflict between intrinsic motivation and the use of extrinsic constraints like evaluation and reward). But the Common Core and creativity can, with a bit of ingenuity, be made to work together in a mutually productive synthesis.

FROM CONCEPTS TO CLASSROOM

Here are some central ideas to guide teachers planning English Language Arts lessons that will foster creativity *and* help students acquire the skills and knowledge that are outlined in the Common Core ELA Standards:

1. Something we talk about often in this book is the importance of intrinsic motivation. Intrinsic motivation is closely associated with creativity. The fact that people are more creative when they do things that they find interesting or personally meaningful will probably not come as a surprise, but even if intrinsic motivation did not increase creativity it would still be important. We want students to find meaning, value, interest, and sometimes even passion in what and how they learn. When students are engaged in a task with intrinsic interest, they are not only more likely to be creative; they are also learning more. This is one of many ways in which learning for creativity and learning for content knowledge (aka Common Core State Standards) go hand in hand.

2. Perhaps less obvious than the value of intrinsic motivation is the often detrimental effect of extrinsic motivation. Rewards and anticipated evaluations tend to depress creativity, and they also reduce intrinsic motivation. Sometimes teachers need to use rewards, and often they will need to provide evaluations of students' work. However, teachers can aim to not make rewards and evaluations any more salient than they must be. If students are already interested in a task, adding bribes (that is, rewards) will do nothing to enhance their work; they are already motivated. It can take away something important, though—the intrinsic motivation students bring to the task.

3. Extrinsic motivation can be problematic and we try not to encourage it in our students. However, there are times when extrinsic constraints are necessary in teaching, especially in the form of feedback (evaluation). Some things to bear in mind when providing feedback on students' work are:
   a. It is important to focus your critical evaluation on the specific work students have done for the assignment and not on the students' overall abilities. This holds true whether your feedback is positive or negative. Focusing on students' specific work rather than overall ability has less of a negative impact on creativity.
   b. When praising student work, teachers should emphasize the effort students put into it rather than any underlying ability. This will lead to more effort on the part of students in future

assignments. It can also lead to students being less focused on appearing to be "smart" (which can lead students to avoid challenges and to give up more easily when confronted with difficult tasks). Praising student effort rather than student ability supports both creativity *and* the acquisition of skills and content knowledge; we will discuss this idea in more detail in Chapter 6.

c. It isn't necessary for everything students do to be evaluated. It's sometimes okay to let students know that a writing assignment must be completed but that it *won't* be evaluated. When doing this, it is important to let students know in advance that there will be no evaluation or grading, or else they may assume their work will be evaluated and thus lose the benefit. This technique allows students freedom to try out new things, explore possibilities, take chances, or risk failure—all of which are associated with creativity. Teachers need to understand that this may encourage intrinsic motivation in some students, but may result in other students expending a minimum amount of effort. We shouldn't penalize the students who make good use of these ungraded assignments to punish those who will use them unwisely. After all, most assignments will still be graded—this isn't *carte blanche* permission to relax. But even an occasional assignment of this nature can make a world of difference to students who *are* intrinsically motivated. If everything is evaluated, it is hard to maintain one's intrinsic motivation, and we don't want to turn joyful learning into nothing but drudgery.

4. Brainstorming is a tool designed to produce divergent thinking. There are other, similar techniques to elicit divergent thinking, such as Talents Unlimited's "productive thinking" mantra: "generate many, varied, and unusual ideas" (Newman, 2005, p. 85). These types of activities can be used in many different ways in the classroom. For example, students may be asked to brainstorm what they know about a topic before reading about it. This can help activate students' prior knowledge as well as letting teachers learn the preexisting knowledge (and misunderstandings) that students may already bring to the table. Brainstorming is also useful before students start writing to help them generate lists of possible ideas. Divergent thinking techniques can be used in some manner in almost any lesson. Divergent thinking is associated with creativity, but beyond that, it is a way to help connect students' preexisting knowledge with what they are about to learn. This link is essential if new content knowledge is going to be understood and retained. This

is another example of a way to use an important creative thinking tool—namely, divergent thinking—in the service of learning the content knowledge and skills that constitute the ELA Common Core.

5. Many of the ELA Standards have to do with students analyzing different types of writing assignments, from poetry and prose to nonfiction and essays. Such activities may not always be labeled analysis, as in the case of "separating fact, opinion, and reasoned judgment," which involves extensive analysis, although this specific label is not used in the Standards. In general, however, analytic thinking is central to English Language Arts. One useful and powerful method to help students learn how to analyze their reading assignments is to have students create the kinds of writings they will eventually be reading and analyzing. This type of work will help students better understand the structure of the things they will be asked to analyze, and it will also encourage students' intrinsic motivation by putting them in the role of writers. Any time students are creating their own writings (regardless of type), it adds their creativity to the lesson.

CONCLUDING THOUGHTS

Creativity and the Common Core can work well together in English Language Arts. Yes, there are times when promoting one may interfere with the other, such as when we provide feedback to promote skill development and in doing so lead students to focus (at least temporarily) on extrinsic constraints. But there are even more times when thinking creatively about a piece of writing can also produce a better understanding of the (Common Core–based) skills one needs to produce such writing—not to mention the need for those Core-based skills, if students are to become truly creative writers. Combining and mixing activities in which students themselves *produce* (create) the kinds of writing they are also evaluating generates powerful synergies that can lead to both improved skills and enhanced creativity.

In the next chapter we turn our focus to mathematics and ways to further both students' understanding of mathematical concepts and their creativity as mathematical thinkers.

CHAPTER 5

Practical Applications 2

Creative Lessons and Insights in Mathematics

Vignette 1: Mathematical Permutations and Combinations

Imagine a teacher, Ms. Jones, who teaches a multiage 4th- and 5th-grade class and has repeatedly found that her students have difficulty engaging with and understanding various math concepts and principles. Permutations and combinations are particularly challenging concepts for her students. Typically, she would teach these concepts through an initial demonstration, practice worksheets, and examples from their text. However, inspired by a video she watched of a team of Rutgers University researchers working with elementary students (Harvard-Smithsonian Center for Astrophysics [HSCA], 2000), she modified her standard lesson format to try to engage her students in a more realistic application of the mathematical ideas. Instead of demonstrating the concepts of combination and permutation and then having her students use worksheets to practice on similar problems, she started the unit on combination and permutations by saying: "Imagine you have an opportunity to open a pizza restaurant in our school cafeteria. The restaurant can serve pizzas with up to four different toppings. You need to make a poster advertising how many different pizza choices are available for your customers. Working with a partner, figure out how many different options your customers have. You can use whatever you want to demonstrate your solution, including any materials we have in this classroom or that you own. You can do this activity any way you would like as long as you both agree that your demonstration best represents your thinking and solutions. We'll be sharing our solutions with each other in a couple of days." Just as the researchers from Rutgers observed (HSCA, 2000), Ms. Jones noticed a high level of engagement and deep levels of mathematical discourse amongst her students. By the end of an hour of work, each pair came up with at least one novel representation of the problem that differed from all other groups. Some students made cutouts of life-size pizzas and toppings, others made succinct charts using a binary counting system to represent the different combinations, some made drawings, and still others used Legos to represent the various combinations.

Common Core State Standards Addressed

➤ CCSS.Math.Practice.MP1. Make sense of problems and persevere in solving them.
➤ CCSS.Math.Practice.MP2. Reason abstractly and quantitatively.
➤ CCSS.Math.Practice.MP3. Construct viable arguments and critique the reasoning of others.
➤ CCSS.Math.Practice.MP4. Model with mathematics.
➤ CCSS.Math.Practice.MP5. Use appropriate tools strategically. (NGACPB & CCSSO, 2014c)

Analysis. The above scenario describes how a teacher used a realistic context to encourage both students' deeper mathematical reasoning and creative thinking simultaneously. As we discussed in Chapter 3, when teachers use academic subject matter as a means for attaining realistic and meaningful goals (rather than as an end in itself), students are more likely to see the relevance of the subject matter. As a result, they are more willing to engage with it. This engagement, in turn, helps ensure that they will develop a deeper understanding of what they are learning, and addresses several key math-practice standards. By providing a pizza-topping analogy, the teacher is helping students contextualize the problem and work with the more abstract concepts of permutation and combination (MP2, MP4). Doing so provides students with "entry points to [a] solution," helps them "analyze givens, constraints, relationships, and goals," and encourages them to model their solutions using available resources, such as concrete objects and images (MP1, MP4, MP5). Also, by requiring students to share their solutions, the teacher provides her students with opportunities to practice constructing, communicating, and critiquing mathematical arguments (MP3).

Given that the teacher invites her students to share their solutions in their own way, she is providing an opportunity for them to practice articulating their mini-c ideas and to develop them into little-c contributions. Recall that the transition from mini-c to little-c requires providing feedback to help ensure that student ideas are both original and task appropriate. Let's imagine two students who share an original vision for how to represent the different combinations—for example, perhaps they develop an interpretive dance about the different pizza toppings. If they do not accurately represent all the possible combinations, they would need feedback from the teacher (or their peers) to make the necessary corrections. Similarly, a pair of students who developed an accurate representation of the combination but simply copied an earlier example would benefit from additional encouragement and support to come up with a more novel representation.

Summary. Vignette 1 describes a situation that can occur at any grade level. When students are introduced to abstract mathematical concepts and principles they may have difficulty understanding (and thus engaging with) the problems. We are not saying that students do not need to learn how to reason abstractly; rather, students sometimes need a realistic or more concrete context in order to engage with a problem. By introducing combination and permutation through a "pizza problem," Ms. Jones was able to provide a context that all her students could understand. In addition to engaging students, the context and guidelines she established produced an activity that also covered many of the Common Core math practice standards.

Vignette 2: Applying Mathematical Knowledge in New Situations

---

Imagine two teachers. The first, Ms. Hendrix, is a 2nd-grade teacher, and the second, Mr. Herman, is an 8th-grade math teacher. Although they teach students from different grade levels, both had a similar discovery when teaching math. They found that most of their students could solve math problems effectively that were nearly identical to those modeled by the teacher. However, these same students would quickly become lost if they were either asked to solve a slightly different problem with the same strategy or solve a similar problem using a different strategy. In short, the students had difficulty both transferring new knowledge to old problems and applying old knowledge to new problems. In the case of Ms. Hendrix's 2nd-graders, when she demonstrated the "borrowing" strategy for solving double column subtraction problems—such as $26 - 17 = 9$—her students continued to use the borrowing strategy (e.g., "Borrow 10 from the 20, add it to 6 . . . this equals 16, then take away 7, which equals 9") in every subtraction problem they encountered. Students who typically created original and effective solutions to subtraction problems they faced in board and dice games consistently relied on borrowing when the problems were set in double columns, even in cases in which borrowing was clearly not the best strategy. Similarly, Mr. Herman's 8th-grade algebra students would only use the particular strategy he demonstrated to solve word problems, rather than come up with their own algebraic expressions to solve the problem (even though they seemed capable of doing so). In short, both the elementary and middle school students could effectively memorize and reproduce strategies, but failed to believe they could develop their own new and appropriate (i.e., mini-c) solutions to such problems—even though they seemed capable of doing so. As a result, both teachers discovered a simple strategy that helped their students share their mini-c ideas that, in turn, sometimes led to little-c contributions and a deeper understanding of mathematics. When a problem was introduced, students were asked to think of as many ways as possible to solve the problem. Both teachers were amazed at how such a simple request could increase the number of novel solutions to problems.

Common Core State Standards Addressed

> ➤ CCSS.Math.Practice.MP1. Make sense of problems and persevere in solving them.
> ➤ CCSS.Math.Practice.MP2. Reason abstractly and quantitatively.
> ➤ CCSS.Math.Practice.MP4. Model with mathematics.
> ➤ CCSS.Math.Practice.MP7. Look for and make use of structure.
> ➤ CCSS.Math.Practice.MP8. Look for and express regularity in repeated reasoning. (NGACPB & CCSSO, 2014c)

Analysis. The two teachers independently discovered an important insight about practice and habits of mind (Baer, 1994, 1996). Simply stated, what you practice is what you get. If problem-solving behaviors have been practiced so much that they become automatic, then it can eventually become difficult to see other ways of solving similar problems. As Sternberg (2006) has argued, creativity is a habit. Unless students are encouraged and expected to develop the habit of creative thinking in their mathematical problem solving, it is unlikely that they will later demonstrate it. Fortunately, students are still in the process of developing their mathematical habits. As such, by simply encouraging students to practice solving problems in as many ways as possible when introducing new material, students can develop the habit of using their divergent thinking abilities while remaining mathematically accurate. Indeed, when students are invited or expected to be creative when solving problems, they are more likely to do so.

Asking students to come up with as many ways to solve a problem as possible (rather than simply finding one way that works) is a slight modification to how one teaches, but it can go a long way in encouraging students to express their creative ideas and deepen their mathematical reasoning. This simple change can create the conditions whereby students are also more likely to address several core math standards. For instance, when students are asked to go beyond reproducing what has already been demonstrated, they will likely spend more time with problems rather than "simply jumping into a solution attempt" (MP1). Students are also provided with opportunities to use flexibly different properties of operations, model problems symbolically, and come up with their own personally meaningful ways of solving problems (MP2, MP3), rather than simply reproducing strategies or algorithms that the teacher has demonstrated. Asking students to come up with many different ways to solve a problem also requires that they look for patterns and the underlying structure of problems in addition to looking for general methods and shortcuts (MP7 & MP8). This is perhaps best illustrated by using an actual classroom example (adapted from Niu & Zhou, 2010).

A 3rd-grade math teacher in China asked her students to come up with as many solutions as possible to the following problem:

> The distance of the railroad track running between the south and north side of a city is 357 kilometers. An express train starts from the north; simultaneously, a local train starts from the south. The two trains run toward each other. In 3 hours, the two trains meet. The speed of the express train is 79 kilometers per hour. How many kilometers per hour less does the local train travel on average as compared to the express train?

In response, students provided a vast array of solutions to this problem. Below are a few examples, adapted from the 15 unique solutions presented in Niu and Zhou (2010, pp. 277–278).

- *Student 1*: $[357 - (79 \times 3)] / 3] = [357 - 237] / 3 = 120 / 3 = 40$ (km). The local train travels 40 km/hour. We already know that the express train travels 79 km/hour; therefore, 79 - 40 = 39 (km). The local train travels 39 km less per hour on average than the express train.
- *Student 2*: $79 - (357 / 3 - 79) = 39$ (km).
- *Student 4*: Suppose the local train travels x km per hour, $(79 + x) \times 3 = 357$; $237 + 3x = 357$; $3x = 120$; $x = 40$; $79 - 40 = 39$ (km).
- *Student 5:* Suppose the local train travels x km per hour, $(3x = 357 - 79 \times 3)$.
- *Student 7:* Suppose the local train travels x km per hour, $79 + x = 357 / 3$.
- *Student 9:* Suppose the local train travels x km less than the express train per hour, $(79 - x) \times 3 + 79 \times 3 = 357$; $474 - 3x = 357$; $3x = 117$; $x = 39$ (km).
- *Student 13:* Suppose the local train travels x km less than the express train per hour, $79 + (79 - x) = 357 / 3$.
- *Student 15:* Suppose the local train travels x km less than the express train per hour, $79 - x = 357 / 3 - 79$.

Here's another example (reported in Levenson, 2011, p. 221). A 6th-grade teacher was reviewing with her students how to multiply decimal fractions. She put the following problem on the board:

___ × ___ = .18

She then asked the class, "What could the missing numbers possibly be?" Several students raised their hands. Before calling on any of them, however, the teacher stated, "There are many possibilities." She then started calling on students. Below is an excerpt from the class discussion that ensued:

Gil: 0.9 times 0.2
Teacher: Good. Another way. There are many ways.
Lolly: 0.6 times 0.3
Teacher: Good. More!
Tammy: 0.90 times 0.20.
Teacher: Would you agree with me that 0.2 and 0.9 is the same [as 0.90 and 0.20]? I want different.
Miri: I'm not sure. What about 9 times 0.02?
Teacher: Nice. Can someone explain what she did?

The teachers in the above examples break free from the prototypical pattern of classroom talk. Mehan (1979), for example, noted that classroom talk typically follows a repeating, IRE pattern. Specifically, teachers ask a question (Initiate), students provide an answer (Respond), and teachers evaluate the correctness of students' responses (Evaluate). Once teachers get a correct response they move on to the next question, repeating the IRE pattern. Of course, not all teachers adhere to this pattern of classroom talk. But it is quite common and often gets passed on from one generation of teachers to the next (Beghetto, 2013). In fact, the IRE pattern of talk is so widespread that children often use it to signify that they are playing "school" (Cazden, 2001). The problem with the IRE pattern is that it encourages rapid convergence on one correct response, rather than inviting students to share and elaborate on their mini-c ideas.

The teachers in the above examples do not adhere to the IRE pattern. Rather, they invite as many responses as possible. This is most evident in the teacher from the second example. She continually paused and invited her students to generate multiple solutions. Prior to calling on the students, she stressed "there are many possibilities." Then, after the first student responded correctly, she again invited additional responses by saying, "Another way. There are many ways." Even after a student provided a second solution she invited, "More." When a student essentially gave the same response, she stressed that she "wanted different." A student tentatively shared an idea and she encouraged it and asked the other students to elaborate on the idea. When teachers simply ask students to come up with and share as many solutions to the problem as possible, they can simultaneously promote creative and mathematical thinking.

Summary. This vignette illustrates two powerfully simple insights. The first pertains to developing the habit of creative thinking. If teachers want their students to think creatively when solving problems, they need to make this expectation explicit and provide ample time to practice developing this habit. The second insight pertains to how, specifically, teachers can encourage creative thinking when asking students to solve problems. One way is to simply ask students to come up with as many ways of solving a problem as they can. Students can then share their various approaches, receive feedback, and learn from one another. This technique is not something that is done occasionally, but rather habitually. It can be done when teachers introduce new problems or mathematical operations, when students are asked to work on practice problems, and when students are assessed on assignments, quizzes, and exams. In this way, creativity and standards-based mathematical learning become a "both/and"—rather than "either/or" learning goal (Beghetto, 2013).

Vignette 3: Using Design Challenges in Mathematics Teaching

Imagine a high school geometry teacher, Ms. Wright, who felt as though she was spending as much time trying to respond to her students' questions of "Why do we have to learn this?" as actually trying to teach them geometry. Year after year students would let her know that they failed to see the application of geometry to life, that her class was "boring" or "worthless," and that they couldn't possibly see the relevance of what they were learning. She, too, failed to see the value in having her students simply memorize and reproduce proofs. She realized that the way she had been teaching simply wasn't working for her or her students. Inspired by watching a video about problem-based learning on Edutopia (www.edutopia.org), she redesigned her geometry class. She still taught the same content, but in a different way. Specifically, she started the class by letting students know that they would be working on a design challenge. Working in teams of four, students would design a school of the future. She specified that their schools needed to be "green" (ecologically friendly), "economical" (using quality but affordable materials), "functional" (able to accommodate the changing needs of teaching and learning), and "beautiful" (aesthetically pleasing). She found an easy-to-use "freeware" Computer Aided Design (CAD) program that her students used to design their schools. With a simple phone call to a local architecture firm, she established a lasting partnership with some of the architects there. The firm agreed to having one of their architects visit the class (either face-to-face or via videochat) and discuss the constraints of the project (using vivid examples). The architect would then return twice during the class to provide technical support, and then join a panel of experts at the end of the class to judge the most creative designs. The firm also agreed to display the winning designs in their foyer. Not only has this new challenge resulted in a more engaging and enjoyable teaching experience for Ms. Wright, but her section of the class has become so popular that each year it has a waiting list for student enrollments.

Common Core State Standards Addressed

➤ CCSS.Math.Practice.MP4. Model with mathematics.
➤ CCSS.Math.Practice.MP5. Use appropriate tools strategically.
➤ CCSS.Math.Practice.MP6. Attend to precision. (NGACPB & CCSSO, 2014c)

Analysis. Establishing a meaningful context is one of the most important things teachers can do to help ensure that students understand the reasons why they are learning a particular academic subject matter. When students can see the relevance to the real world, they can grasp the rationale for learning academic subjects that might otherwise seem too abstract or obscure. Having the goal of designing a "school of the future" casts core geometry principles as a means for attaining that goal. This is very different from the approach that Ms. Wright used to take. This new project brings the concepts of geometry to life.

As we will discuss in Chapter 6, project-based learning can serve as an effective curricular vehicle to simultaneously support meaningful learning, creative thinking, and the attainment of Common Core State Standards. In the case of this vignette, the school design project provided students with an opportunity to generate their own unique solutions to this design problem (MP4) and use a variety of tools to solve the problem, including design software, calculators, sketches, and models (MP5). Throughout this process, students also had to focus on communicating their ideas to expert audiences in a precise and accurate manner. In order to best convey this information, they had to choose appropriate symbols and units of measurement, label their sketches and draft designs clearly, and display their final models (MP6).

Summary. This vignette provides an example of how teachers can move away from representing academic subject matter as an end in itself and instead help students to reconceptualize it as a means to another (perhaps more practical) end. Doing so not only results in more meaningful and engaging lessons for students, but also presents students with opportunities to imagine themselves in future professional roles and identities—professionals who use mathematics as part of their problem-solving process. In this way, math becomes a vehicle for possibility thinking. It allows students to develop and express their ideas in the context of real-world problems. They are exposed to the kinds of professional activities that use mathematical tools to solve problems, which can lead them to imagine eventually assuming such professional roles and identities.

HOW TO TEACH FOR CREATIVITY WHILE TEACHING THE MATHEMATICS COMMON CORE

As is the case with any constraint, standards can sometimes feel too limiting to allow for student and teacher creativity. However, constraints are a common and often necessary part of creative expression. As we have discussed, creativity can be defined in a classroom context as constrained originality (see Chapters 1 and 2). Thinking about creativity in this way can help teachers recognize that the Common Core State Standards in math provide the constraints. The challenge, then, is finding ways that students can develop and express original thinking within those constraints. The combination of originality and mathematics may not, at first, seem feasible. One reason is because in math, as opposed to some other subject areas, there is often only one correct solution. That being said, there are often multiple ways to reach that solution and countless ways to formulate mathematically related problems. In this way, math provides at least two areas where teachers can infuse creativity. The first area is in how they design activities that require mathematical solutions and the second is in how students attempt to solve such problems.

When taking a closer look at the Common Core State Standards, teachers will see that the standards have been separated into two main categories: *Standards for Mathematical Practice* and *Standards for Mathematical Content*. We will first discuss each category on its own, noting how creativity can be infused in and across these two types of standards. We will then share ideas for how the two types of standards can be connected and combined with creativity.

One way to think of the standards for mathematical practice (MP) is that they are more general standards, which cut across content and grade levels. These are the processes and proficiencies that teachers from kindergarten to high school can incorporate into their everyday math teaching. Below are the standards for mathematical practice:

Standards for Mathematical Practice (NGACPB & CCSSO, 2014c, pp. 6–8)

1. *Make sense of problems and persevere in solving them.* Mathematically proficient students start by explaining to themselves the meaning of a problem and looking for entry points to its solution. They analyze givens, constraints, relationships, and goals. They make conjectures about the form and meaning of the solution and plan a solution pathway rather than simply jumping into a solution attempt. They consider analogous problems and try special cases and simpler forms of the original problem in order to gain insight into its solution. They monitor and evaluate their progress and change course if necessary. Older students might, depending on the context of the problem, transform algebraic expressions or change the viewing window on their graphing calculator to get the information they need. Mathematically proficient students can explain correspondences between equations, verbal descriptions, tables, and graphs or draw diagrams of important features and relationships, graph data, and search for regularity or trends. Younger students might rely on using concrete objects or pictures to help conceptualize and solve a problem. Mathematically proficient students check their answers to problems using a different method, and they continually ask themselves, "Does this make sense?" They can understand the approaches of others to solving complex problems and identify correspondences between different approaches.

2. *Reason abstractly and quantitatively.* Mathematically proficient students make sense of quantities and their relationships in problem situations. They bring two complementary abilities to bear on problems involving quantitative relationships: the ability to *decontextualize*—to abstract a given situation and represent it symbolically and manipulate the representing symbols as if they have a life of their own, without necessarily attending to their referents—and the ability to *contextualize*, to pause as needed during the manipulation process in order to probe into the referents for the symbols involved. Quantitative reasoning entails habits of creating a coherent representation of the problem at hand; considering the units involved; attending to the meaning of quantities, not just how to compute them; and knowing and flexibly using different properties of operations and objects.

3. *Construct viable arguments and critique the reasoning of others.* Mathematically proficient students understand and use stated assumptions, definitions, and previously established results in constructing arguments. They make conjectures and build a logical progression of statements to explore the truth of their conjectures. They are able to analyze situations by breaking them into cases, and can recognize and use counterexamples. They justify their conclusions,

communicate them to others, and respond to the arguments of others. They reason inductively about data, making plausible arguments that take into account the context from which the data arose. Mathematically proficient students are also able to compare the effectiveness of two plausible arguments, distinguish correct logic or reasoning from that which is flawed, and—if there is a flaw in an argument—explain what it is. Elementary students can construct arguments using concrete referents such as objects, drawings, diagrams, and actions. Such arguments can make sense and be correct, even though they are not generalized or made formal until later grades. Later, students learn to determine domains to which an argument applies. Students at all grades can listen or read the arguments of others, decide whether they make sense, and ask useful questions to clarify or improve the arguments.

4. *Model with mathematics.* Mathematically proficient students can apply the mathematics they know to solve problems arising in everyday life, society, and the workplace. In early grades, this might be as simple as writing an addition equation to describe a situation. In middle grades, a student might apply proportional reasoning to plan a school event or analyze a problem in the community. By high school, a student might use geometry to solve a design problem or use a function to describe how one quantity of interest depends on another. Mathematically proficient students who can apply what they know are comfortable making assumptions and approximations to simplify a complicated situation, realizing that these may need revision later. They are able to identify important quantities in a practical situation and map their relationships using such tools as diagrams, two-way tables, graphs, flowcharts, and formulas. They can analyze those relationships mathematically to draw conclusions. They routinely interpret their mathematical results in the context of the situation and reflect on whether the results make sense, possibly improving the model if it has not served its purpose.

5. *Use appropriate tools strategically.* Mathematically proficient students consider the available tools when solving a mathematical problem. These tools might include pencil and paper, concrete models, a ruler, a protractor, a calculator, a spreadsheet, a computer algebra system, a statistical package, or dynamic geometry software. Proficient students are sufficiently familiar with tools appropriate for their grade or course to make sound decisions about when each of these tools might be helpful, recognizing both the insight to be gained and their limitations. For example, mathematically proficient high school students analyze graphs of functions and solutions generated using a graphing calculator. They detect possible errors by strategically using estimation and other mathematical knowledge. When making mathematical models, they

know that technology can enable them to visualize the results of varying assumptions, explore consequences, and compare predictions with data. Mathematically proficient students at various grade levels are able to identify relevant external mathematical resources, such as digital content located on a website, and use them to pose or solve problems. They are able to use technological tools to explore and deepen their understanding of concepts.

6. *Attend to precision.* Mathematically proficient students try to communicate precisely to others. They try to use clear definitions in discussion with others and in their own reasoning. They state the meaning of the symbols they choose, including using the equal sign consistently and appropriately. They are careful about specifying units of measure, and labeling axes to clarify the correspondence with quantities in a problem. They calculate accurately and efficiently, express numerical answers with a degree of precision appropriate for the problem context. In the elementary grades, students give carefully formulated explanations to each other. By the time they reach high school they have learned to examine claims and make explicit use of definitions.

7. *Look for and make use of structure.* Mathematically proficient students look closely to discern a pattern or structure. Young students, for example, might notice that three and seven more is the same amount as seven and three more, or they may sort a collection of shapes according to how many sides the shapes have. Later, students will see 7×8 equals the well-remembered $7 \times 5 + 7 \times 3$, in preparation for learning about the distributive property. In the expression $x^2 + 9x + 14$, older students can see the 14 as 2×7 and the 9 as $2 + 7$. They recognize the significance of an existing line in a geometric figure and can use the strategy of drawing an auxiliary line for solving problems. They also can step back for an overview and shift perspective. They can see complicated things, such as some algebraic expressions, as single objects or as being composed of several objects. For example, they can see $5 - 3(x-y)^2$ as 5 minus a positive number times a square and use that to realize that its value cannot be more than 5 for any real numbers x and y.

8. *Look for and express regularity in repeated reasoning.* Mathematically proficient students notice if calculations are repeated, and look both for general methods and for shortcuts. Upper elementary students might notice when dividing 25 by 11 that they are repeating the same calculations over and over again, and conclude they have a repeating decimal. By paying attention to the calculation of slope as they repeatedly check whether points are on the line through (1, 2) with slope 3, middle school students might abstract the equation $(y-2)/(x-1) = 3$. Noticing the regularity in the way terms cancel when

expanding $(x-1)(x+1)$, $(x-1)(x^2+x+1)$, and $(x-1)(x^3+x^2+x+1)$ might lead them to the general formula for the sum of a geometric series. As they work to solve a problem, mathematically proficient students maintain oversight of the process, while attending to the details. They continually evaluate the reasonableness of their intermediate results.

The eight MP standards, described above, provide key constraints that can be incorporated into almost any math activity and used across any grade level (as illustrated in the opening vignettes). Now, let's take a look at a summary of the math content (MC) standards:

The math content standards focus on mathematical procedures and specific math content that students should understand as they progress through the various grade levels. One way to think of the MC standards is that they are organized or nested in four levels. Specific content standards (e.g., count to 100 by ones and tens) are clustered together in related themes (e.g., Use place value understanding and properties of operations to perform multi-digit arithmetic), which are nested under broader content categories, called *Domains* (e.g., know number names and the count sequence). The domains are also nested in specific grade levels (e.g., kindergarten, 6th grade, high school).

At first glance, all the nested standards, domains, and clusters can be somewhat overwhelming. We would, therefore, recommend spending time becoming familiar with the most general level: the various grade content domains with their corresponding grade levels (listed below). Spend time working at this level when thinking about and planning lessons—recognizing that the particular standards and clusters of standards represent concrete, grade-level-appropriate examples of these more general concepts.

Math Content Domains and Grade Levels

Elementary School

- Counting and Cardinality (K)
- Operations and Algebraic Thinking (K–5)
- Number and Operations in Base Ten (K–5)
- Geometry (K–HS)
- Measurement and Data (K–5; HS)
- Number and Operations—Fractions (3–5)

Middle School

- Ratios and Proportional Relationships (6–7)
- The Number System (6–8)
- Expressions and Equations (6–8)

- Geometry (6–8)
- Statistics and Probability (6–8)
- Functions (8)

High School

- Functions (8, HS)
- Algebra (HS)
- Number and Quantity (HS)
- Modeling (HS)
- Geometry (HS)
- Measurement and Data (HS)
- Statistics and Probability (HS) (NGACPB & CCSSO, 2014c)

The MC standards listed above provide the highest level of constraints on what students are expected to learn across grade levels. Still, teachers can work creatively within these constraints. They can seek opportunities to promote mathematical understanding while simultaneously developing their students' creative potential. One way to do this is to combine the various MC and MP standards in new and meaningful ways.

The combination and reorganization of seemingly disparate information into new ideas, information, or products is a key process involved in creative problem solving (Finke, Ward, & Smith, 1992; Mumford, Medeiros, & Partlow, 2012). Mumford et al. (2012), for instance, have described a creative process model that has combination at its core. More specifically, once a problem has been defined (e.g., developing a creative math lesson that includes both math practice and math content standards) and information has been gathered and organized (e.g., listing various required standards and math learning activities), these can then be combined in novel ways that, in turn, can be evaluated, implemented, and monitored. Moreover, as Mumford and his colleagues have explained, the most original outcomes often are produced from the combination of the most diverse concepts or elements.

Rothenberg (1991) explored the concept of merging two directly opposite ideas together. He dubbed this process Janusian thinking, named after the two-faced Roman god Janus. Rothenberg (1996) argued that Big-C creators, such as Nobel Prize winners, were more likely to use Janusian thinking. Instilling in your students the ability to join together seemingly disparate concepts can be a lifelong skill.

There are various ways that teachers can use conceptual combination to develop potentially creative lessons. One way is to start with an existing math lesson and combine it with a different topic to generate a new lesson. Beghetto has used this approach in professional development workshops with teachers. Teachers start out the creative lesson planning workshop by identifying an existing lesson they want to modify and then combine it with some seemingly unrelated theme or topic of interest. For example, in one workshop, teachers first spent time in a children's museum. Prior to viewing the various exhibits, they had to first identify a standards-based lesson that they would be teaching, but wanted to rework. They then had time to identify and explore exhibits in the children's museum that caught their interest. As soon as an exhibit caught their interest, they would spend time exploring it and jotting down ideas about how some aspect of the exhibit might inform or be combined with the lesson they wanted to rework. After spending 30–40 minutes in the museum, the teachers identified at least one idea that they wanted to elaborate on to rework. They then spent time sharing their ideas with small groups of colleagues who represented various grade levels, receiving input and suggestions from them to further refine their ideas. Finally, they had time to refine their lessons independently by incorporating the feedback they received from their peers. A few of these lesson ideas are included at the end of this chapter, as well as at the end of Chapter 4.

Teachers need not attend a workshop or have groups of colleagues provide feedback to effectively use conceptual combination. The museum activity is something teachers can modify and do on their own, and subsequently get feedback from one or two trusted colleagues. They can visit online and virtual museums (e.g., www.exploratorium.edu) or sites like Edutopia (www.edutopia.org) to explore and get ideas. There are also online resources—such as the National Library of Virtual Manipulatives (nlvm. usu.edu)—that teachers can incorporate into their lessons. In the "From Concepts to Classrooms" box at the end of this chapter, we describe and provide examples of a four-step lesson-development process that teachers can use to develop new lessons or modify existing ones.

CONCLUDING THOUGHTS

Returning to the opening vignettes, we can see that the various lessons share several qualities. Specifically, they represent projects of varying duration (longer and shorter) and type (simulation and design projects), cover both MP and MC standards, come with multiple and unique problems, and creatively use subject matter as a means to another end. It is our hope that these examples and lesson ideas have sparked ideas for your own classroom.

The next chapter (Chapter 6) provides additional information for how you might incorporate creativity into your lessons—including a more detailed discussion of the types of instructional activities that can be used (e.g., design projects and simulations), how you might combine various academic subjects with Common Core State Standards, and ideas for assessing creativity and Common Core learning while teaching in diverse settings.

FROM CONCEPTS TO CLASSROOM

Let's take a closer look at a simple four-step process for how teachers can generate lessons that combine creativity with Common Core MP and MC standards.

Step 1. Select the number of grade-level-appropriate content domains you want to address. Two or three should provide enough divergence to generate an original lesson. Let's use Grade 6 as an example. The Common Core math standards outline five domains for this level. When selecting content domains you can select them based on what you want to cover or randomly select them (using dice or simply by picking a number). You'll be surprised at the kinds of creative and quality lessons that can be generated from randomly combining standards. Let's say you pick #1 (*Ratios and Proportional Relationships*) and #4 (*Geometry*) from the Grade 6 domains. Recall that specific content standards are nested in each domain and specific content standards are thematically clustered. In Grade 6, the Ratios and Proportional Relationships domain includes one thematic cluster (i.e., "understand ratio concepts and use ratio reasoning to solve problems") with three specific content standards. One of the three content standards is "Use ratio and rate reasoning to solve real-world and mathematical problems." Even more specifically, it asks that students "Solve unit rate problems including those involving unit pricing and constant speed." Grade 6 Geometry includes four specific content standards clustered under the theme of "Solve real-world and mathematical problems involving area, surface area, and volume." One of the four content standards is "Find the area of right triangles, other triangles, special quadrilaterals, and polygons by composing into rectangles or decomposing into triangles and other shapes" (NGACPB & CCSSO, 2014c).

Step 2. Select Mathematical Practice Standards. Recall that the Common Core outlines eight MP standards (regardless of grade level). We again suggest selecting two or three MP standards to blend with content standards. As with the content standards, you can pick these intentionally or randomly. Let's say you pick MP standards 5 ("use appropriate tools strategically") and 6 ("attend to precision"). Now it's time to generate some ideas for activities that can emerge from combining your Content and MP standards.

Step 3. Decide on the duration. When generating some ideas, it might be helpful to first decide on the duration of your project. How much time do you have to devote to this lesson? Creative lessons can range from a single day to many weeks. When possible, it is a good idea to try to have a mix of shorter and longer projects—introducing and revisiting various standards. For simplicity, the matrix uses long (10 or more weeks) and short (1–3 days).

Step 4. Decide on the type of activity. One aspect of designing engaging and creative lessons is that the lesson should focus on using the MC and MP standards as a means to another end (rather than as an end in themselves). So, rather than design an activity that stops with students calculating area, for instance, the activity should have students calculating area to reach some other goal. Deciding on the type of goal informs the nature of the activity you will design. Again, for simplicity, the matrix focuses on two types of activities: simulations and design projects (described further in Chapter 6). Both simulations and real-world projects can be used in shorter and longer lessons. You can create mini-projects that last a couple of days or long-term projects that last 6 months or more. The same can be said for simulations. The difference between simulations and real-world projects is that simulations engage students in situations that can have real-world or imaginative elements, or some combination of the two (such as Example #1 below, the disaster response team project). Design projects, on the other hand, require students to design something—a product or a solution—that makes a contribution beyond the walls of the classroom (such as Example #2 below, the tomato garden project).

Two examples, using the information from above, may help to illustrate how using these four steps can result in designing new and creative math lessons (using the same MC and MP content but varying the duration and nature of the activity).

Example 1: Short Simulation—Disaster Response Team

Students are provided with the following situation (adapted from Howard County Public School System, 2013, Available at grade6commoncoremath. wikispaces.hcpss.org/Unit+4+Geometry).

> "Today, we received word of a truck carrying toxic chemicals tipping over on a rural highway outside a major U.S. city. As a result, tons of toxic chemicals have spilled onto the highway. Your team of researchers has been contacted to investigate this chemical spill and report your findings to government officials. Specifically, you are tasked with determining the amount of area that was initially affected by the spill and figuring out how long it may take before the nearby city is impacted by the toxic gases, which are traveling at a

constant rate. You will be asked to report your analysis and findings to the government researchers. Use the available tools (graph paper, rulers, calculators, and computer) to solve this problem. Precision is the key. You will need to communicate your findings clearly and precisely, using mathematically accurate language and symbols. You will also need to use your knowledge of how to determine the area of a polygon to help solve this problem. Ensure that your final aerial map demonstrates how you have determined the total area of the chemical spill, and how soon the toxins will reach the nearby city. Create as many evacuation methods and routes as you can for the people in the nearby city. Your team will need to present and justify your findings. The lives of hundreds of thousands of people are in your hands!"

This lesson is a short simulation that combines MC6.RP3b, MC6G1 with MP5 and MP6 (NGACPB & CCSSO, 2014c) and provides students with opportunities to create multiple solutions to problems. Importantly, it allows students to use academic content standards as a means to another end (solving the simulation).

Example 2: Long-term Design Project—Tomato Garden

Each year the 6th grade hosts a spaghetti dinner fundraiser. The company that provides the tomato sauce recently had a recall for food contamination, and the students decided that they wanted to make sauce out of freshly grown tomatoes. The dinner is scheduled to occur in 6 months and the principal has agreed to provide them with a $100 school project loan and space to grow the tomatoes. The students are expected to reimburse the school for the initial $100 start-up cost. Throughout the project they will be addressing various MC and MP content standards, including the ones described in the first example. For instance, they will need to geometrically map out and calculate the area of a polygon to figure out how many tomatoes they can plant. They will also need to understand ratios and solve problems using ratios. For example, they may need to ask questions such as: "If it takes 3 weeks to grow 50 tomatoes, how many tomatoes can be grown in 20 weeks?"; "If it takes 25 tomatoes to make enough pasta sauce to feed 30 people, how many tomatoes are needed to make enough sauce to feed 90 people?"; "How many weeks of growing tomatoes will it take before we have enough tomatoes to feed the 90 people at the spaghetti dinner fundraiser?"; and "If it costs us $1 to make a pasta plate and we want to raise $250 with only 90 people attending the dinner, what do we need to charge for each plate to make $250?" Along the way they will need to use appropriate tools strategically (MP5) and attend to precision (MP6). As with the simulation, this longer-term design project puts MC and MP standards to work. Students can be encouraged to come up with creative solutions for a variety of the problems they will encounter. These may include figuring out the best arrangement for the tomato plants in the space provided, or the tomato sauce recipe that makes the best sauce most efficiently. In this way, the subject matter learning serves as a means to another end, which will result in a real-world contribution that extends beyond the classroom walls.

CHAPTER 6

Where Do We Go from Here?

Bringing together creativity and the Common Core in the previous five chapters has led us in many interesting directions, and we've covered a great deal of territory in showing how teachers can both teach for creativity and teach to the Common Core. Although we've acknowledged some places where the two are indeed in conflict (such as the need sometimes to use rewards and evaluations to promote learning, even though these may have negative short-term consequences for student creativity), we've noted far more opportunities for synergies.

There are many places where promoting creativity can lead to increased Common Core skill and knowledge acquisition, such as (1) the use of brainstorming to activate students' prior knowledge and reveal possible misconceptions and (2) the importance of fostering intrinsic motivation, to boost both creativity and content learning. There are also many places where increasing Common Core–based knowledge and skills will promote more creative thinking, such as (1) giving students opportunities to actually do the kinds of creative writing that they are learning how to read and analyze and (2) acknowledging the fact that creativity must be based on broad and deep content knowledge in many domains.

These two concurrent goals—developing students' knowledge and understanding of Common Core–based skills and content, and promoting student creativity in all subject areas by teaching them creative thinking skills, fostering a creativity-friendly environment, and giving them opportunities for creative expression—can also be *converging* goals. This idea is crucial for teachers who want to nurture students' creativity but who also recognize the need to adapt instruction to meet the requirements of the Common Core.

In this concluding chapter we will provide additional information for how teachers can incorporate creativity into their teaching—including some suggestions regarding the use of instructional activities, ideas for teaching creativity across the curriculum, and suggestions for assessing creativity. We will then close the chapter with a brief synthesis of some key tips drawn from the previous chapters and provide a list of resources for readers who are interested in learning more about creativity, both within and outside of the classroom.

WHAT ARE THE BEST INSTRUCTIONAL TECHNIQUES
FOR PROMOTING CREATIVITY?

There is no such thing as "instant creativity" or surefire techniques that will magically produce creative results; if there were, we'd be writing that book and selling it for twice the price of this one. There are, however, ways to incorporate creativity in almost any Common Core lesson. We have devoted much of this book to providing and discussing examples of how to do so. Many of the ideas we have discussed have focused on making slight changes to one's existing instructional practices. We feel this is one of the best and most feasible ways to incorporate creativity in the Common Core curriculum. That being said, we want to comment on a common question we sometimes get from teachers: "What is the *best* instructional technique to use when trying to incorporate creativity in the curriculum?" This is an important and persistent question, particularly given that each school year seems to bring some new (or, at least, repackaged) instructional approach or technique that sweeps across K–12 education—ranging from using screencasts to "flip the classroom" (i.e., teachers creating screencasts of direct content instruction to free up class time for work on more engaging and in-depth projects and activities) to taking a "design-based" approach to learning (i.e., presenting students with a design challenge, such as "design a sustainable school garden that can provide food for the local homeless shelter").

Do these approaches promote creativity and learning? Are some better than others? Should teachers adopt these approaches in their teaching? In response to these questions, we would suggest that it isn't the techniques that are most important, but how and why those techniques are used. We sometimes forget that a simple stick of chalk and a chalkboard, in the hands of a capable teacher, is all that is needed to teach a profoundly creative math lesson. A lesson in which students share their own unique approaches to a problem, challenge one another, and end up deepening their own, their peers', and maybe even their teacher's mathematic understanding can come in many forms and flow from many different teaching approaches.

As we have discussed from the outset of this book, the development of creativity is fueled by domain knowledge. This knowledge can be made more meaningful when students have an opportunity to creatively engage with academic content. So, again, it's not the technique that is most important, but rather the principled use of techniques. This is good news for school administrators and teachers because it frees them from thinking that they must chase after the latest instructional fads and techniques and allows them instead to focus their attention on key instructional principles that can guide the selection, use, and development of approaches that make the most sense for their particular instructional goals and school context.

When it comes to teaching for creativity and meaningful standards-based learning, a key instructional principle is what can be called the "means to another end" (MAE) principle. This principle applied to this book's topic states that creativity and subject matter learning do not serve as ends in themselves, but as means to some other instructional end (or goal). This principle is at the heart of instructional techniques that use cases, scenarios, problems, inquiry, and design projects as vehicles for putting students' (and sometimes teachers') learning and creativity to work.

As with any instructional technique, however, if students do not receive adequate guidance, then MAE-based techniques would be less likely to result in increased content knowledge (see Kirschner, Sweller, & Clark, 2006). Fortunately, researchers have identified conditions that can increase the likelihood that MAE-based techniques will result in meaningful learning. Schmidt et al. (2009), for instance, highlight four conditions that seem necessary for instructional approaches, such as problem-based learning, to contribute to student learning. Those conditions include: (1) compelling problems or issues of inquiry that evoke students' curiosity and serve as relatable and relevant focal points for students' learning; (2) focused interactions among students, working in small groups, which require students to activate and elaborate on their prior knowledge and develop positive working relationships and accountability among one another; (3) a knowledgeable teacher who actively engages students in didactic conversations and provides necessary guidance and support; and (4) teachers having the time and content-based materials necessary to support, structure, and check students' self-directed learning.

Taken together, teachers can combine the MAE principle with the four conditions of success to develop creative Common Core lessons that range in scope from 1 hour (or less), such as the short "disaster response simulation" described in Chapter 5, to more ambitious and expansive projects that can last several weeks or even an entire school year, such as the "tomato garden design project" (also described in Chapter 5). In sum, developing creative and engaging Common Core lessons is less about technique and more about taking a principled approach to designing creative lessons that fit one's particular goals, resources, and context.

CREATIVITY ACROSS THE CURRICULUM

Creativity can happen anywhere. It can occur in any domain, in any class, in any subject, and can come from any student. It does not only happen in art class or English class. It is something that can (and should) be happening in *every* class, in *every* subject, and at *every* grade level. We are not saying that creativity should always be the primary goal. We are not suggesting teachers should promote creative classroom disruptions by their students—at least not most of the time! Although we believe there are many creative ways to teach and learn facts of all kinds—such as dates of historical events, multiplication tables, and the details of Mendel's experiments with pea plants—we are not suggesting or in any way promoting creativity as a *replacement* for factual knowledge. We are, however, arguing that there are creative ways to interpret most facts and creative possibilities for applying those facts in diverse contexts.

Just as teachers have long understood that writing isn't only for English class, teachers today need to understand that creativity shouldn't be taught and promoted only in a single class. Research has shown us that creativity varies widely across domains (Baer & Kaufman, 2005; Kaufman & Baer, 2002, 2004b, 2005; Kaufman, Cole, & Baer, 2009). Students who are very creative in the ways in which they think about math may be much less creative in the ways that they think about language (just as teachers who are very creative at designing lesson plans in language arts may not be creative at writing poetry, sculpting, or cooking—or even designing lesson plans in mathematics). Creativity isn't some skill or set of skills that one can bring out and apply regardless of content. Creativity within a domain is part of the very nature of that domain; it is intimately connected to the content of that domain. Creativity should not be confused with expertise—the two may overlap to some degree but are nonetheless very different—and yet creativity and expertise are similar in one important way: Both tend to be rather domain-specific. Just as we would not assume that someone who knows a great deal about the novels of Toni Morrison will also know a great deal about the moons of Jupiter, we should also not assume that students who are very creative in one type of activity will be creative in all kinds of activities.

There is a great deal of evidence to suggest that doing things to promote student creativity in a domain will in fact increase student creativity within that domain. That's the good news. The bad news is that promoting creativity in one domain does very little to increase creativity in other domains (Baer, 1993, 1994, 1996). To increase student creativity in multiple areas, we need to teach for creativity in all those subjects in which we want to promote student creativity. This is just as true of creativity as it is of learning the kinds of skills and knowledge outlined in the Common Core. We wouldn't expect helping students learn things in English language arts would necessarily improve their understanding of mathematics (or vice versa). We must teach for creativity in all subjects, just as we must teach for skill and knowledge acquisition in all subjects. Having a stand-alone, content-free Creativity Class makes no more sense than having a stand-alone, content-free Expertise Class. We need to teach for creativity in every subject, not just one or a few.

ASSESSING CREATIVITY AND COMMON CORE LEARNING

There is no getting around a fundamental truism in education: That which is assessed is that which matters most. In fact, if creativity is absent from classroom-based assessments, then it cannot be said that creativity has been incorporated into a classroom (regardless of how often one stresses the importance of creativity or how many creative learning activities one uses). Indeed, as Guilford (1950) has cautioned, "Let us remember . . . the kinds of examinations we give really set the objectives for the students, no matter what objectives we may have stated" (p. 448).

Following Guilford, we can say that unless we include expectations for creativity in assignments and assessments—and actually reward creative thinking in those assessments—the message is quite clear: Creativity really doesn't matter. How might teachers assess creativity as part of standards-based learning? At first blush, this may seem like a nearly impossible question to answer. A quick look at the creativity literature will reveal a vast array of creativity assessment methods and techniques (see Kaufman, Plucker, & Baer, 2008; Plucker & Makel, 2010). Most of these techniques, however, have been developed for the purpose of creativity research or for selecting students for specialized gifted and talented programs. Teachers will be hard-pressed to find ready-made assessments that they can seamlessly drop into their curriculum and use to assess creativity and Common Core subject matter simultaneously.

A closer look at the literature, however, will reveal that creativity researchers have started developing assessments that combine creativity and academic learning. Elena Grigorenko and her colleagues (Grigorenko, Jarvin, Tan, & Sternberg, 2008), for instance, have started developing assessments with the goal of measuring both academic and creative proficiency. These assessments are being developed and used primarily by researchers. However, Grigorenko and her colleagues (2008) note that once these assessments have been developed, they can be broken down into teachable exercises and activities that teachers can use to nurture student creativity and academic learning. Others have proposed ways that teachers can modify their existing classroom assessments and have provided suggestions for how teachers might develop rubrics to monitor students' developing creative and academic proficiency (Beghetto, 2013; Brookhart, 2013).

One of our students modified a rubric she found on the ASCD website (www.ascd.org/publications/educational-leadership/oct04/vol62/num02/ The-Writing-Rubric.aspx) for an activity in which upper elementary students conducted a mock interview of an important historical figure. The original rubric had categories like Content, Organization, Word Choice, Sentence Structure, and a four-point scale for each (Saddler & Andrade, 2004). She adapted the original rubric and added one important piece: a Creativity rating (see Table 6.1).

Table 6.1. Adapted Rubric, Including Creativity Criteria

	4	3	2	1
Creativity	My interview questions are interesting and original, not the kinds of questions everyone else would ask. I ask questions that bring my character to life. My interview brings out many interesting things about my character's life.	My interview makes my character interesting to readers. At least one of my questions is interesting and original, and my interview brings out several interesting things about my character's life.	My interview brings out one or two interesting things about my character's life that would make it interesting to a reader, but parts of it are very dull.	My interview is dull and boring. It doesn't bring my character to life and there is nothing in it to make the reader interested in my character.

This is the kind of adaptation of existing lessons and existing assessment practices that will allow the assessment of creativity along with the assessment of other objectives that might more closely align with the curriculum (and the Common Core State Standards).

With respect to working with existing assessment practices, the first step is to identify what aspects of one's existing assessment practices can be modified. One way to do so is to ask questions such as, "Does this assessment require convergence on one solution? If so, how might I modify this assessment so that students are asked to try to find one or more original ways to arrive at or represent that solution? If it doesn't require convergence on one solution, how can I modify this assessment so that students are expected to provide multiple unique and appropriate solutions and multiple ways at arriving at those solutions?" In both cases, teachers would be assessing whether students can generate accurate and unique (i.e., not previously modeled) responses. Many good teachers already do this in many of their assessments. The key is doing it more systematically and helping students to be aware that such responses are not simply correct but also creative (at least in the context of that particular class or assignment).

Teachers can incorporate aspects of divergent thinking techniques in their assessments to evaluate whether students can demonstrate their understanding in unique and accurate ways. One example is a version of the "Zwicky Box" developed by Fritz Zwicky (1969), the Swiss Astronomer. This technique, sometimes called Morphological Synthesis, involves creating a matrix of elements that represent some key academic concept or topic.

Elements of a narrative can serve as an example. A teacher can list the various elements of a narrative, including setting, conflict, main characters, and point of view. Then, to assess whether students understand and can apply these narrative elements, teachers can ask students to fill out several examples under each element and then randomly select one from each category to use in writing a unique narrative. Teachers would assess whether students could provide accurate examples of these elements and whether they could apply these elements in an original story. Table 6.2 provides an example of what a completed table might look like. Based on this table a student could, for instance, write a first-person story about two 6th-grade friends who have to deal with a zombie invasion in their classroom.

Another example is SCAMPER (Eberle, 1996). SCAMPER is an acronym that stands for Substitute, Combine, Adapt, Modify, Put to another use, Eliminate, and Reverse. SCAMPER can be used to assess students' ability to come up with novel representations of their understanding. When teaching math, for instance, teachers could provide students with an algebraic expression and have them generate a solution. Then, using that solution, teachers could have students work in *reverse* to demonstrate what different types of algebraic formulations could result in that same solution. In writing, for instance, teachers can have students read a published story and then *eliminate* a key scene or character and write how the story changes as a result.

In addition to modifying existing assessments, teachers can also create a two-part holistic rubric that can be used to simultaneously assess developing levels of academic and creative proficiency (see Beghetto, 2013, for a detailed description). Holistic rubrics focus on overall quality, proficiency, and demonstration of skills and are well-suited for assessing learning activities that require a creative response (Mertler, 2001). By adding levels of creative proficiency to rubrics, teachers can incorporate creativity into their existing assessments of academic subject matter. In this way, rubrics can help teachers and students to identify different levels of growing

Table 6.2. Zwicky Box

Setting	Conflict	Main Characters	Point of View
Haunted House	Friends fighting	Two 6th-grade friends	First person
Ranch	Tornado	Teachers	Second person
China	Nuclear war	Group of friends	Third person
Mars	Lost at sea	Space aliens	Naïve narrator
Classroom	Zombies	Barn animals	Stream of consciousness

proficiency. Table 6.3 is an example of how creativity can be included in a mathematical problem-solving rubric (adapted from Beghetto, 2013).

Teachers (and students) can develop and use a rubric, like the one in Table 6.3, to simultaneously assess creativity and mathematical problem solving. The academic side of the rubric would provide examples of increasing levels of proficiency in mathematical problem solving—ranging from emerging proficiency to accomplished (and even expert) proficiency. Emerging proficiency would be represented in students using inappropriate approaches or using appropriate methods but making many mistakes. Accomplished proficiency would be represented in students using appropriate methods, providing sound explanations for their approach, and making no mistakes. Expert proficiency would serve as an example and challenge to students—representing examples of solving highly complex problems using more specialized analytic techniques.

Table 6.3. Mathematical Problem Solving—Example Rubric

Level of Proficiency	DESCRIPTION	
	Academic	Creative
4— Expert	Able to solve highly complex problems using more advanced or specialized mathematical knowledge.	Student solves a particularly complex problem using novel methods that might be used by more advanced students or professional mathematicians.
3— Accomplished	Uses appropriate methods. Makes no mistakes. Sound explanations of thinking.	The student approaches a problem from a highly unique yet task-appropriate perspective.
2— Developing	Uses appropriate methods. Makes few mistakes. Offers explanations of thinking.	The student uses a novel and accurate approach to solving the problem.
1— Emerging	Uses an inappropriate approach. Makes mistakes. Offers no explanation of thinking.	The student tries using a previously modeled method that is new to them (but not new to others) or uses a novel but mathematically inaccurate approach.
0— No Attempt	No response or attempt.	Task not attempted.

Note: Academic and creative proficiency descriptions adapted from Mertler (2001) and Grigorenko et al. (2008).

The creative side of the rubric would similarly assess and provide examples of increasing creative proficiency in mathematical problem solving. Emerging creative proficiency refers to students who simply use an approach that someone else showed them. Accomplished creative proficiency would be represented in students who are solving a problem using a highly unique—yet task-appropriate—method. Expert creative proficiency would provide examples of how particularly complex problems have been solved using novel methods that might be used by professional mathematicians.

In sum, teachers can draw on these assessment examples and descriptions to incorporate creativity more systematically into their existing assessments and to start developing their own assessments and rubrics. Developing one's own assessments requires ongoing refinement. Classroom assessments, like rubrics, can be strengthened by inviting colleagues and, when possible, other subject matter experts to provide feedback on how the different levels of proficiency are being described and represented in the rubric. Teachers can also develop their own understanding of growing proficiency by reading the existing academic and creativity literature.

In creativity, for example, there are various models that outline different levels of creative development (Cohen, 1989; Taylor, 1959) and types of creative contributions (e.g., Sternberg, Kaufman, & Pretz, 2002). Teachers can also test and refine their assessments and rubrics by having students and colleagues practice using them to assess samples of student work and then discuss whether they are able to establish consistent scores. Ideally, a rubric can be used by almost anyone to consistently assess differing levels of performance. It's also important for teachers to monitor how well student performance on these types of classroom assessments aligns with other indicators of learning and creative performance.

SYNTHESIS OF KEY CONCEPTS AND TIPS

- Teach and promote divergent thinking through the use of brainstorming and other idea-generating techniques. These can be used when students are planning how to conceptualize a problem, when students are developing possible problem-solving approaches, or when teachers are introducing a new topic.
- Encourage intrinsic motivation and downplay extrinsic constraints, rewards, and evaluations to the largest extent possible.
- When using praise, focus on student effort, not on how "smart" students are. Encourage students to think of being smart as a muscle that can be exercised and made stronger, not something they simply have (or lack).

- Use creative thinking and problem solving as ways to help students explore and deepen their understanding and retention of important ideas and facts.
- Teach for creativity in all subject areas, not just a few.
- Emphasize that creativity can emerge at all levels—from beginner to genius.
- Help students appreciate that their own personally meaningful insights "count" as being creative.
- Don't neglect your own creativity. Remember that your creativity—as expressed in your teaching, your interactions with your students, or in other venues of your life—is important.

RESOURCES FOR LEARNING MORE ABOUT CREATIVITY

Recommended Creativity-Related Books from the Last Few Years

Baer, J., & Kaufman, J. C. (2013). *Being creative inside* and *outside the classroom.* Rotterdam, The Netherlands: Sense Publishers.

Beghetto, R. A. (2013). *Killing ideas softly? The promise and perils of creativity in the classroom.* Charlotte, NC: Information Age Publishing.

Beghetto, R. A., & Kaufman, J. C. (Eds.). (2010). *Nurturing creativity in the classroom.* New York, NY: Cambridge University Press.

Craft, A. (2011). *Creativity and education futures: Learning in a digital age.* Stoke-on-Trent, England: Trentham.

Daniels, S., & Peters, D. A. (2013). *Raising creative kids.* Scottsdale, AZ: Great Potential Press.

Daniels, S., & Piechowski, M. (Eds) (2009). *Living with intensity: Understanding the sensitivity, excitability, and emotional development of gifted children, adolescents, and adults.* Scottsdale, AZ: Great Potential Press.

Gregerson, M., Kaufman, J. C., & Snyder, H. (Eds.). (2013). *Teaching creatively and teaching creativity.* New York, NY: Springer Science.

Kaufman, J. C. (2009). *Creativity 101.* New York, NY: Springer.

Kaufman, S. B. (2013). *Ungifted.* New York, NY: Basic Books.

Piirto, J. (2011). *Creativity for 21st Century skills: How to embed creativity into the curriculum.* Rotterdam, The Netherlands: Sense Publishers.

Piirto, J. (Ed.). (2013). *Organic creativity in the classroom.* Scottsdale, AZ: Great Potential Press.

Plucker, J. A., & Callahan, C. M. (Eds.). *Critical issues and practices in gifted education: What the research says* (2nd ed.). Waco, TX: Prufrock Press.

Runco, M. A. (2014). *Creativity: Theories and themes: Research, development, and practice* (2nd ed.). San Diego, CA: Academic Press.

Saracho, O. N. (Ed.). (2012). *Contemporary perspectives on research in creativity in early childhood education.* Charlotte, NC: Information Age Publishing.

Sawyer, R. K. (Ed.). (2011). *Structure and improvisation in creative teaching.* New York, NY: Cambridge University Press.

Sawyer, R. K. (2012). *Explaining creativity: The science of human innovation.* Oxford, England: Oxford University Press.

Simonton, D. K. (2009). *Genius 101.* New York, NY: Springer.

Sternberg, R. J. (2010). *College admissions for the 21st century.* Cambridge, MA: Harvard University Press.

Tan, A. G. (Ed.). (2007). *Creativity: A handbook for teachers.* Singapore: World Scientific.

A Few Older Recommended Creativity-Related Books

Csikszentmihalyi, M. (1996). *Creativity.* New York, NY: HarperCollins.

Getzels, J. W., & Jackson, P. W. (1962). *Creativity and intelligence: Explorations with gifted students.* New York, NY: Wiley.

Sternberg, R. J., & Lubart, T. I. (1995). *Defying the crowd.* New York, NY: Free Press.

Torrance, E. P. (1966). *Guiding creative talent.* New York, NY: Prentice-Hall.

Creativity-Related Journals

Creativity Research Journal (Taylor & Francis)
Empirical Studies of the Arts (Baywood Publishing)
Gifted Child Quarterly (National Association for Gifted Children)
High Ability Studies (Routledge)
International Journal of Creativity and Thinking Skills (Korean Association for Thinking Development)
Journal of Creative Behavior (Creative Educational Foundation)
Psychology of Aesthetics, Creativity, and the Arts (American Psychological Association)
Roeper Review (Roeper School)
Thinking Skills and Creativity (Elsevier)

Creativity Related Organizations

American Creativity Association (www.aca.cloverpad.org)
Center for Creative Learning (www.creativelearning.com)
Creative Education Foundation (www.creativeeducationfoundation.org)
Creative Problem Solving Group (www.cpsb.com)
Society for the Psychology of Aesthetics, Creativity, and the Arts—
    Division 10 of the American Psychological Association
    (www.div10.org)

References

Aljughaiman, A., & Mowrer-Reynolds, E. (2005). Teachers' conceptions of creativity and creative students. *Journal of Creative Behavior, 39*, 17–34.

Amabile, T. M. (1979). Effects of external evaluation on artistic creativity. *Journal of Personality and Social Psychology, 37*, 221–233.

Amabile, T. M. (1982). Children's artistic creativity: Detrimental effects of competition in a field setting. *Personality & Social Psychology Bulletin, 8*, 573–578.

Amabile, T. M. (1983). *The social psychology of creativity*. New York, NY: Springer.

Amabile, T. M. (1996). *Creativity in context*. Boulder, CO: Westview Press.

Amabile, T. M., DeJong, W., & Lepper, M. R. (1976). Effects of externally-imposed deadlines on subsequent intrinsic motivation. *Journal of Personality and Social Psychology, 34*, 92–98.

Amabile, T. M., Goldfarb, P., & Brackfield, S. C. (1990). Social influences on creativity: Evaluation, coaction, and surveillance. *Creativity Research Journal, 3*, 6–21.

Amabile, T. M., Hennessey, B. A., & Grossman, B. S. (1986). Social influences on creativity: The effects of contracted-for reward. *Journal of Personality and Social Psychology, 50*, 14–23.

Amabile, T. M., Hill, K. G., Hennessey, B. A., & Tighe, E. M. (1994). The work preference inventory: Assessing intrinsic and extrinsic motivational orientations. *Journal of Personality and Social Psychology, 66*, 950–967.

American Federation of Teachers [AFT]. (2013). AFT poll of 800 teachers finds strong support for Common Core Standards and a moratorium on stakes for new assessments until everything is aligned (Press Release). Retrieved from www.aft.org/newspubs/press/2013/050313.cfm

Ames, C. (1992). Classrooms: Goals, structures, and student motivation. *Journal of Educational Psychology, 84*, 261–271.

Baer, J. (1993). *Divergent thinking and creativity: A task-specific approach*. Hillsdale, NJ: Lawrence Erlbaum.

Baer, J. (1994). Divergent thinking is not a general trait: A multi-domain training experiment. *Creativity Research Journal, 7*, 35–46.

Baer, J. (1996). The effects of task-specific divergent-thinking training. *Journal of Creative Behavior, 30*, 183–187.

Baer, J. (1997). The hidden costs of rewards and evaluation: Who gets hurt, and what teachers can do. *Focus on Education, 41*, 24–27.

Baer, J. (1998). Gender differences in the effects of extrinsic motivation on creativity. *Journal of Creative Behavior, 32*, 18–37.

Baer, J., & Garrett, T. (2010). Teaching for creativity in an era of content standards and accountability. In R. A. Beghetto & J. C. Kaufman (Eds.), *Nurturing creativity in the classroom: Between chaos and conformity* (pp. 6–23). New York, NY: Cambridge University Press.

Baer, J., & Kaufman, J. C. (2005). Bridging generality and specificity: The Amusement Park Theoretical (APT) model of creativity. *Roeper Review, 27,* 158–163.

Baer, J., & Kaufman, J. C. (2006). Creativity in English-speaking countries. In J. C. Kaufman & R. J. Sternberg (Eds.), *International handbook of creativity* (pp. 10–38). New York, NY: Cambridge University Press.

Baer, J., & Kaufman, J. C. (2012). *Being creative inside and outside the classroom.* Rotterdam, The Netherlands: Sense Publishers.

Bandura, A. (1997). *Self-efficacy: The exercise of control.* New York, NY: Freeman.

Barron, F. (1955). The disposition towards originality. *Journal of Abnormal and Social Psychology, 51,* 478–485.

Beghetto, R. A. (2005). Does assessment kill student creativity? *The Educational Forum, 69,* 254–263.

Beghetto, R. A. (2006). Creative self-efficacy: Correlates in middle and secondary students. *Creativity Research Journal, 18,* 447–457.

Beghetto, R. A. (2007). Ideational code-switching: Walking the talk about supporting student creativity in the classroom. *Roeper Review, 29,* 265–270.

Beghetto, R. A. (2009). Correlates of intellectual risk taking in elementary school science. *Journal of Research in Science Teaching, 46,* 210–223.

Beghetto, R. A. (2013). *Killing ideas softly? The promise and perils of creativity in the classroom.* Charlotte, NC: Information Age Publishing.

Beghetto, R. A. (2014). Creative mortification: An initial exploration. *Psychology of Aesthetics, Creativity, and the Arts, 8*(3), 266–276.

Beghetto, R. A., & Kaufman, J. C. (2007). Toward a broader conception of creativity: A case for "mini-c" creativity. *Psychology of Aesthetics, Creativity, and the Arts, 1,* 13–79.

Beghetto, R. A., & Kaufman, J. C. (2013). Creativity: Five fundamental insights that every educator should know. *Educational Leadership, 70,* 10–15.

Beghetto, R. A., & Kaufman, J. C. (2014). Classroom contexts for creativity. *High Ability Studies,25*(1), 53–69.

Berliner, D. C. (2011). Narrowing curriculum, assessments, and conceptions of what it means to be smart in the U.S. schools: Creaticide by design. In D. Ambrose & R. J. Sternberg (Eds.), *How dogmatic beliefs harm creativity and higher-level thinking* (pp. 79–93). New York, NY: Routledge.

Bidwell, A. (2014, March 6). The politics of the common core. *U.S. News and World Report.* Retrieved from www.usnews.com/news/special-reports/a-guide-to-common-core/articles/2014/03/06/the-politics-of-common-core

Bloom, B.S. (Ed.). (1956). *Taxonomy of educational objectives.* New York, NY: David McKay.

Brookhart, S. M. (2013). Assessing creativity. *Educational Leadership, 70,* 28–34.

Brown, A. C., & Schulten, K. (2013, January). News and 'news analysis': Navigating fact and opinion in the Times. *New York Times.* Retrieved from learning.blogs.nytimes.com/2013/01/17/news-and-news-analysis-navigating -fact-and-opinion-in-the-times

Byron, K., & Khazanchi, S. (2012). Rewards and creative performance: A meta-analytic test of theoretically derived hypotheses. *Psychological Bulletin, 138,* 809–830.

Cazden, C. B. (2001). *Classroom discourse: The language of teaching and learning* (2nd ed.). Portsmouth, NH: Heinemann.

Chan, D. W., & Chan, L.-K. (1999). Implicit theories of creativity: Teachers' perception of student characteristics in Hong Kong. *Creativity Research Journal, 12*(3), 185–195.

Cho, Y., Chung, H. Y., Choi, K., Seo, C., & Baek, E. (2013). The emergence of student creativity in classroom settings: A case study of elementary schools in Korea. *Journal of Creative Behavior, 47,* 152–169.

Clifford, M. M. (1991). Risk taking: Theoretical, empirical, and educational considerations. *Educational Psychologist, 26,* 263–297.

Cohen, L. M. (1989). A continuum of adaptive creative behaviors. *Creativity Research Journal, 2,* 169–183.

Cropley, D. H., Cropley, A. J., Kaufman, J. C., & Runco, M. A. (Eds.). (2010). *The dark side of creativity.* New York, NY: Cambridge University Press.

Cropley, D. H., Kaufman, J. C., & Cropley, A. J. (2008). Malevolent creativity: A functional model of creativity in terrorism and crime. *Creativity Research Journal, 20,* 105–115.

Csikszentmihalyi, M. (1999). Implications of a systems perspective for the study of creativity. In R. J. Sternberg (Ed.), *Handbook of Creativity* (pp. 313–335). New York, NY: Cambridge University Press.

Davies, D., Jindal-Snape, D., Collier, C., Digby, R., Hay, P., & Howe, A. (2012). Creative learning environments in education: A systematic literature review. *Thinking Skills and Creativity, 8,* 80–91.

Dweck, C. S. (1999). *Self-theories: Their role in motivation, personality, and development.* Philadelphia, PA: Psychology Press/Taylor & Francis.

Dweck, C. S. (2006). *Mindset.* New York, NY: Random House.

Eberle, B. (1996). *Scamper: Creative games and activities for imagination development.* Austin, TX: Prufrock Press.

Egan, T. (2014, March 22). Creativity vs. quants. *The New York Times.* Retrieved from www.nytimes.com/2014/03/22/opinion/egan-creativity-vs-quants.html

Eisenberger, R., Pierce, W., & Cameron, J. (1999). Effects of reward on intrinsic motivation—Negative, neutral, and positive: Comment on Deci, Koestner, and Ryan. *Psychological Bulletin, 125*(6), 677–691.

Eisenberger, R., & Shanock, L. (2003). Rewards, intrinsic motivation, and creativity: A case study of conceptual and methodological isolation. *Creativity Research Journal, 15,* 121–130.

Ericsson, K. A. (Ed.). (1996). *The road to expert performance: Empirical evidence from the arts and sciences, sports, and games.* Mahwah, NJ: Erlbaum.

Finke, R. A., Ward, T. B., & Smith, S. M. (1992). *Creative cognition: Theory, research, and applications.* Cambridge, MA: MIT Press.

Forgeard, M. J. C., & Mecklenburg, A. C. (2013). The two dimensions of motivation and a reciprocal model of the creative process. *Review of General Psychology, 17,* 255–266.

Glaveanu, V. P. (2013). Rewriting the language of creativity: The five A's framework. *Review of General Psychology, 17,* 69–81.

Greenwald, A. G., & Banaji, M. R. (1995). Implicit social cognition: Attitudes, self-esteem, and stereotypes. *Psychological Review, 102,* 4–27.

Grigorenko, E. L., Jarvin, L., Tan, M., & Sternberg, R. J. (2008). Something new in the garden: Assessing creativity in academic domains. *Psychology Science, 50,* 295.

Guilford, J. P. (1950). Creativity. *American Psychologist, 5,* 444–454.

Güncer, B., & Oral, G. (1993). Relationship between creativity and nonconformity to school discipline as perceived by teachers of Turkish elementary school children, by controlling for their grade and sex. *Journal of Instructional Psychology, 20,* 208–214.

Harvard-Smithsonian Center for Astrophysics (HSCA, Producer). (2000). *Private universe project in mathematics.* Retrieved from www.learner.org/resources /series120.html

Hennessey, B. A. (2010a). The creativity-motivation connection. In J. C. Kaufman & R. J. Sternberg (Eds.), *The Cambridge handbook of creativity* (pp. 342–365). New York, NY: Cambridge University Press.

Hennessey, B. A. (2010b). Intrinsic motivation and creativity in the classroom: Have we come full circle. In J. C. Kaufman & R. A. Beghetto (Eds.), *Nurturing creativity in the classroom* (pp. 329–361). New York, NY: Cambridge University Press.

Hennessey, B. A., & Amabile, T. M. (1988). Storytelling: A method for assessing children's creativity. *Journal of Creative Behavior, 22,* 235–246.

Hennessey, B. A., & Zbikowski, S. M. (1993). Immunizing children against the negative effects of reward: A further examination of intrinsic motivation training techniques. *Creativity Research Journal, 6,* 297–307.

Iyengar, S. S., & Lepper, M. R. (1999). Rethinking the value of choice: A cultural perspective on intrinsic motivation. *Journal of Personality and Social Psychology, 76,* 349–366.

Kaufman, J. C. (2002). Narrative and paradigmatic thinking styles in creative writing and journalism students. *Journal of Creative Behavior, 36,* 201–220.

Kaufman, J. C. (2009). *Creativity 101.* New York, NY: Springer.

Kaufman, J. C. (Ed.) (2014). *Creativity and mental illness.* New York, NY: Cambridge University Press.

Kaufman, J. C., & Baer, J. (2002). Could Steven Spielberg manage the Yankees?: Creative thinking in different domains. *Korean Journal of Thinking & Problem Solving, 12,* 5–15.

Kaufman, J. C., & Baer, J. (2004a). The amusement park theoretical (APT) model of creativity. *Korean Journal of Thinking and Problem Solving, 14,* 15–25.

Kaufman, J. C., & Baer, J. (2004b). Hawking's haiku, Madonna's math. In R. J. Sternberg, E. L. Grigorenko, & J. L. Singer (Eds.), *Creativity: From potential to realization* (pp. 3–20). Washington, DC: American Psychological Association.

Kaufman, J. C., & Baer, J., (2005). The amusement park theory of creativity. In J. C. Kaufman & J. Baer (Eds.), *Creativity across domains: Faces of the muse* (pp. 321–328). Mahwah, NJ: Lawrence Erlbaum.

Kaufman, J. C., & Beghetto, R. A. (2009). Beyond big and little: The Four C model of creativity. *Review of General Psychology, 13*, 1–12.

Kaufman, J. C., & Beghetto, R. A. (2013a). Do people recognize the Four Cs? Examining layperson conceptions of creativity. *Psychology of Aesthetics, Creativity, and the Arts, 7*, 229–236.

Kaufman, J. C., & Beghetto, R. A. (2013b). In praise of Clark Kent: Creative metacognition and the importance of teaching kids when (not) to be creative. *Roeper Review, 35*, 155–165.

Kaufman, J. C., Beghetto, R. A., & Baer, J. (2010). Finding young Paul Robesons: Exploring the question of creative polymathy. In R. J. Sternberg & D. D. Preiss (Eds.), *Innovations in educational psychology: Perspectives on learning, teaching and human development* (pp. 141–162). New York, NY: Springer.

Kaufman, J. C., Cole, J. C., & Baer, J. (2009). The construct of creativity: A structural model for self-reported creativity ratings. *Journal of Creative Behavior, 43*, 119–134.

Kaufman, J. C., Plucker, J. A., & Baer, J. (2008). *Essentials of creativity assessment.* New York, NY: John Wiley & Sons.

Kirschner, P. A., Sweller, J., & Clark, R. E. (2006). Why minimal guidance during instruction does not work: An analysis of the failure of constructivist, discovery, problem-based, experiential, and inquiry-based teaching. *Educational Psychologist, 41*, 75–86.

Kruglanski, A. W., Friedman, I., & Zeevi, G. (1971). The effects of extrinsic incentive on some qualitative aspects of task performance. *Journal of Personality, 39*, 606–617.

Kyllonen, P. C., Walters, A. M., & Kaufman, J. C. (2005). Noncognitive constructs and their assessment in graduate education. *Educational Assessment, 10*, 153–184.

Lepper, M. R., & Greene, D. (1975). Turning play into work: Effects of adult surveillance and extrinsic rewards on children's intrinsic motivation. *Journal of Personality and Social Psychology, 31*, 479–486.

Lepper, M. R., & Greene, D. (1978). *The hidden costs of reward: New perspectives on the psychology of human motivation.* Oxford, England: Lawrence Erlbaum.

Levenson, E. (2011). Exploring collective mathematical creativity in elementary school. *Journal of Creative Behavior, 3*, 215–234.

Lewis, M., & Sullivan, M. W. (2005). The development of self-conscious emotion. In A. J. Elliot & C. S. Dweck (Eds.), *Handbook of competence and motivation* (pp. 185–201). New York, NY: Guilford Press.

Lofing, N. (2009, January 10). Davis sixth-grader's science experiment breaks new ground. *Sacramento Bee.* Retrieved from www.sacbee.com/education/v-print/story/1530953.html

Maehr, M. L., & Midgley, C. (1996). *Transforming school cultures: Lives in context.* Boulder, CO: Westview Press.

McNeil, L. M. (2000). Sameness, bureaucracy, and the myth of educational equity: The TAAS system of testing in Texas. *Hispanic Journal of Behavioral Sciences, 22*, 508–523.

Mehan, H. (1979). *Learning lessons: Social organization in the classroom.* Cambridge, MA: Harvard University Press.

Mertler, C. A. (2001). Designing scoring rubrics for your classroom. *Practical Assessment, Research, and Evaluation, 7.* Retrieved from pareonline.net/getvn .asp?v=7&n=25

Midgley, C. (Ed.). (2002). *Goals, goal structures, and patterns of adaptive learning.* Mahwah, NJ: Lawrence Erlbaum.

Mueller, J. S., Goncalo, J. A., & Kamdar, D. (2011). Recognizing creative leadership: Can creative idea expression negatively relate to perceptions of leadership potential? *Journal of Experimental Social Psychology, 47*(2), 494–498.

Mueller, J. S., Melwani, S., & Goncalo, J. A. (2012). The bias against creativity: Why people desire but reject creative ideas. *Psychological Science, 23*(1), 13–17.

Mumford, M. D., Medeiros, K. E., & Partlow, P. J. (2012). Creative thinking: Processes, strategies, and knowledge. *The Journal of Creative Behavior, 46,* 30–47.

National Governors Association Center for Best Practices (NGACBP) & Council of Chief State School Officers (CCSSO). (2014a). *Common Core state standards initiative.* Retrieved from www.corestandards.org

National Governors Association Center for Best Practices (NGACBP) & Council of Chief State School Officers (CCSSO). (2014b). *English language arts standards: Common Core state standards initiative.* Retrieved from www.corestandards .org/ELA-Literacy

National Governors Association Center for Best Practices (NGACBP) & Council of Chief State School Officers (CCSSO). (2014c). *Mathematics standards: Common Core state standards initiative.* Retrieved from www.corestandards.org /Math

Newman, J. L. (2005). Talents and type IIIs: The effects of the Talents Unlimited Model on creative productivity in gifted youngsters. *Roeper Review, 27*(2), 84–90.

Niu, W., & Zhou, J. Z. (2010). Creativity in Chinese mathematics classrooms. In R. A. Beghetto & J. C. Kaufman (Eds.), *Nurturing creativity in the classroom* (pp. 270–288). New York, NY: Cambridge University Press.

Paley, V. G. (2007). HER classic: On listening to what the children say. *Harvard Educational Review, 77,* 152–163.

Plucker, J., Beghetto, R. A., & Dow, G. (2004). Why isn't creativity more important to educational psychologists? Potential, pitfalls, and future directions in creativity research. *Educational Psychologist, 39,* 83–96.

Plucker, J. A., & Makel, M. C. (2010). Assessment of creativity. In J. C. Kaufman & R. J. Sternberg (Eds.), *Cambridge Handbook of Creativity* (pp. 48–73). New York, NY: Cambridge University Press.

Porter, A., McMaken, J., Hwang, J., & Yang, R. (2011). Common Core Standards: The new U.S. intended curriculum. *Educational Researcher, 40,* 103–116.

Reeve, J. M. (2009). Why teachers adopt a controlling motivating style towards students and how they can become more autonomy supportive. *Educational Psychologist, 44,* 159–175.

Reiter-Palmon, R., & Robinson, E. J. (2009). Problem identification and construction: What do we know, what is the future? *The Psychology of Aesthetics, Creativity, and the Arts, 3,* 43–47.

Rhodes, M. (1962). An analysis of creativity. *Phi Delta Kappan, 42,* 305–311.

Rosiek, J., & Beghetto, R. A. (2009). Emotional scaffolding: The emotional and imaginative dimensions of teaching and learning. In P. Schutz & M. Zembylas (Eds.), *Advances in teacher education research* (pp. 175–194). New York, NY: Springer Science+Business Media.

Rothenberg, A. (1991). The Janusian process in psychoanalytic treatment. *Contemporary Psychoanalysis, 27*, 422–453.

Rothenberg, A. (1996). The Janusian process in scientific creativity. *Creativity Research Journal, 9*, 207–231.

Ryan, R. M., & Deci, E. L. (2000). Intrinsic and extrinsic motivations: Classic definitions and new directions. *Contemporary Educational Psychology, 25*, 54–67.

Ryan, R. M., & Deci, E. L. (2006). Self-regulation and the problem of human autonomy: Does psychology need choice, self-determination, and will? *Journal of Personality, 74*, 1557–1586.

Saddler, B., & Andrade, H. (2004). The writing rubric. *Educational Leadership, 62*, 48–52.

Schmidt, H. G., van der Molen, H. T., te Winkel, W. W. R., & Wijnen, W. H. F. W. (2009). Constructivist, problem-based learning does work: A meta-analysis of curricular comparisons involving a single medical school. *Educational Psychologist, 44*, 227–249.

Shepard, L. A. (2009). A brief history of accountability testing, 1965–2007. In K. Ryan & L. Shepard (Eds.), *The future of test-based educational accountability* (pp. 25–46). New York, NY: Routledge.

Simonton, D. K. (1990). *Psychology, science, and history: An introduction to historiometry.* New Haven, CT: Yale University Press.

Simonton, D. K. (1994). *Greatness: Who makes history and why.* New York, NY: Guilford Press.

Simonton, D. K. (2013). What is a creative idea? Little-c versus Big-C creativity. In K. Thomas & J. Chan (Eds.), *Handbook of research on creativity* (pp. 69–83). Northampton, MA: Edward Elgar Publishing.

Standards in your state. (2014). *Common Core state standards initiative.* Retrieved April 21, 2014 from www.corestandards.org/standards-in-your-state

Sternberg, R. J. (1985). *Beyond IQ: A triarchic theory of human intelligence.* New York, NY: Cambridge University Press.

Sternberg, R. J. (2006). The nature of creativity. *Creativity Research Journal, 18*, 87–98.

Sternberg, R. J., & Kaufman, J. C. (2010). Constraints on creativity: Obvious and not so obvious. In J. C. Kaufman & R. J. Sternberg (Eds.), *Cambridge handbook of creativity* (pp. 467–482). New York, NY: Cambridge University Press.

Sternberg, R. J., Kaufman, J. C., & Pretz, J. E. (2002). *The creativity conundrum.* Philadelphia, PA: Psychology Press.

Sternberg, R. J., & Lubart, T. I. (1995). *Defying the crowd: Cultivating creativity in a culture of conformity.* New York, NY: Free Press.

Strauss, V. (2013, July 24). New Common Core tests: Worth the price? *The Washington Post.* Retrieved from www.washingtonpost.com/blogs/answer-sheet /wp/2013/07/24/new-common-core-tests-worth-the-price

Taylor, I. A. (1959). The nature of the creative process. In P. Smith (Ed.), *Creativity* (pp. 521–582). New York, NY: Hastings House.

Torrance, E. P. (1963). *Education and the creative potential*. Minneapolis: University of Minnesota Press.

Tracy, J. L., & Robins, R. W. (2006). Appraisal antecedents of shame and guilt: Support for a theoretical model. *Personality and Social Psychology Bulletin, 32,* 1339–1351.

Vygotsky, L. S. (2004). Play and its role in the mental development of the child. *Journal of Russian and East European Psychology, 5,* 6–18. (Original work published 1967)

Westby, E. L., & Dawson, V. L. (1995). Creativity: Asset or burden in the classroom? *Creativity Research Journal, 8,* 1–10.

Zwicky, F. (1969). *Discovery, invention, research through the morphological approach*. London, England: Macmillan.

Index

"10-year rule," 36

Abstract reasoning, 88
Active cognitive engagement, 4–5
Adoption of Common Core State
    Standards, 1
AFT (American Federation of
    Teachers), 1, 10
Aljughaiman, A., 32
Amabile, T. M., 6–7, 11, 28, 40–42,
    44–45, 57–58, 72
American Federation of Teachers
    (AFT), 1, 10
Ames, C., 45
Amotivation, 41
Amusement Park Theoretical (APT)
    Model, 28–29
Analytic thinking, 78
Andrade, H., 102
Answers that work, 14–15
Applying mathematics, 81–85
Appropriate context for creativity,
    32–33
APT (Amusement Park Theoretical)
    Model, 28–29
Argument, 74, 88–89
Assessing creativity, 102–106
Attitudes toward creativity, 31–32
Autonomy, 49, 51

Background knowledge, 22, 74, 77
Baek, E., 22–23, 25
Baer, J., 3, 6, 28–29, 42, 46, 57, 60, 72,
    82, 101–102
Banaji, M. R., 9, 31
Bandura, A., 25

Barron, F., 21
Beghetto, R. A., 1, 3, 6, 9, 21–27, 30,
    33, 39–40, 45–46, 49, 51–53,
    84–85, 104–105
Berliner, D. C., 2, 11
Bias against creativity, 31–32
Bidwell, A., 1, 10
Big-C creativity, 26–29
Bloom, B. S., 6
Bottom-up initiative, 10
Brackfield, S. C., 45, 57
Brainstorming. *See* Divergent thinking
Brookhart, S. M., 102
Brown, A. C., 63
Byron, K., 43

Cameron, J., 43
"Casey at the Bat," 66
Cazden, C. B., 84
CCSSO (Council of Chief State School
    Officers), 10, 15–17, 40, 43,
    56–57, 63–66, 68–71, 74–75, 80,
    82, 86, 88, 92, 94, 96
Chan, D. W., 32
Chan, L.-K., 32
Chapter overview, 6–7
Character analysis, 60–63
Cho, Y., 22–23, 25
Choi, K., 22–23, 25
Choice and motivation, 50–51
Chung, H. Y., 22–23, 25
Clark, R. E., 100
Clifford, M. M., 45
Cognitive engagement, 4
Cohen, L. M., 106
Cold facts vignette, 20, 23

Cole, J. C., 101
College and Career Readiness Anchor
    Standards. *See also* Common Core
    State Standards
  addressing the standards, 70–75
  listed, 67–70
Collier, C., 34
Combining information, 92
Combining lessons/topics, 92–93
Common Core State Standards. *See
    also* College and Career Readiness
    Anchor Standards
  about, 1
  constraints, 18, 39, 91–92
  ELA-Literacy, 5, 15, 17, 55–57,
      63–71, 75
  math, 6, 15, 80, 82, 86, 91–97
Compare/contrast analysis, 60–63
Compatibility of goals, 1–6, 8–9,
    12–17, 19
Competing goals. *See* Conflicting goals
Competition between students, 45
Componential Model of Creativity, 28
Conflicting goals, 8–10, 12, 37, 56–57,
    67, 73
Constraints of the Common Core State
    Standards, 18, 39, 91–92
Constructing meaning, 4, 24
Content knowledge/skills, 4–5, 12,
    24–25, 35, 37, 98
Context/environment of creativity,
    21–22, 34–35
Convergent thinking, 13
Converging goals, 98
Council of Chief State School Officers.
    See CCSSO (Council of Chief State
    School Officers)
Creative metacognition, 32–34
Creative mortification, 52
Creative writing, 64, 66, 72
Creativity
  across the curriculum, 100–101, 107
  construct, 21
  context/environment and, 21–22,
      34–35
  dimensions, 9
  goal of, 98

instructional techniques, 99–100
  levels, 22–29, 35
  misperceptions, 31–32
  profile, 33
  rating, 102–103
  suppression of, 39–40, 52
  theory application, 29–31
"Creativity time" vignette, 8
Criticism, 30
Cropley, A. J., 3
Cropley, D. H., 3
Csikszentmihalyi, M., 26–27

Davies, D., 34
Dawson, V. L., 31
Deci, E. L., 41, 43, 48–51
DeJong, W., 44
Dialogue in stories, 56–57
Digby, R., 34
Distinguishing among fact, opinion,
    and judgment, 63–65, 74–75
Divergent thinking
  application of, 5–6
  assessing, 103–104, 106
  discussion, 63
  examples, 60–62, 73–74
  misunderstandings about, 13–14,
      16–17
  and prior knowledge, 77–78
  in supporting role, 66
Domain-specific knowledge/skills, 4,
    24, 29–30, 36, 99
Dow, G., 6, 21
Drill-and-kill, 16
Dweck, C. S., 47, 52

Eberle, B., 104
Editorial writing, 64, 74–75
Egan, T., 36
Eisenberger, R., 43
Elaboration-rearticulation-evaluation
    approach, 26
Elementary and Secondary Education
    Act (1965), 10
Elementary level. *See also* Grade
    level; Vignettes and references
    to vignettes: Applying Math

Knowledge; Vignettes and
   references to vignettes: Math
   Permutations
   assessment, 102
   math standards, 88, 90–91
   motivation, 47
   writing activities, 59
Emotions and motivation, 51
Engagement, 47, 59, 73, 76, 79, 85–87
English language arts and literacy
   compare/contrast analysis, 60–63
   creative writing, 64, 66, 72
   dialogue in stories, 56–57
   editorial writing, 64, 74–76
   essay reading/writing, 71–72
   figurative language, 72
   meaning in context, 55–56
   narrative techniques, 56–57
   newspaper content, 63–65, 74–75
   poetry writing, 55–56
   point of view, 72, 75
   reading literature, 15
   reading standards, 67–68
English language arts standards. *See*
   Common Core State Standards:
   ELA-Literacy
Equity in education, 2
Ericsson, K. A., 26
Essay reading/writing, 71–72
Evaluation effect on creativity, 57–59,
   66, 72–73, 76–77
Everyday creativity. *See* Little-c
   creativity
Expected reward. *See* Extrinsic
   motivators
Experiential knowledge, 22, 74, 77
Expert companion, 27
Exploration and evaluation, 26
Extrinsic motivation, 41–45, 57–58,
   72, 76
Extrinsic motivators, 42–45, 47–51,
   57, 106
Extrinsic rewards. *See* Extrinsic
   motivators

Facts focus, 23–24
Feedback, 58, 72, 76–77, 80–81, 85

Figurative language, 72
Finke, R. A., 92
Fitzgerald, F. Scott, 1
Five A's, 21
Fixed ability, 52
Forgeard, M. J. C., 43
Four-C Model of Creativity, 22, 27,
   29–30, 35
Four-P's framework, 21, 29
Friedman, I., 42
Frost, Robert, 55, 71

Garrett, T., 6
Gender and creativity, 72
Genius-level creativity, 26–27
Glaveanu, V. P., 21
Goldfarb, P., 45, 57
Goncalo, J. A., 31
Grade level
   2nd, 81–85
   3rd, 15
   5th, 25, 65–66
   6th, 94–97
   8th, 15, 63–65, 81–85
Greene, D., 42
Greenwald, A. G., 9, 31
Grigorenko, E. L., 29–30, 102, 105
Grossman, B. S., 58
Groth, G., 11
Guilford, J. P., 21, 102
Güncer, B., 32

Habit of creative thinking, 85
Harvard-Smithsonian Center for
   Astrophysics (HSCA), 79
Hay, P., 34
Hennessey, B. A., 11, 40–42, 44–45,
   48–49, 51, 57–58
"Hidden cost of reward," 58
High school, 49, 65, 89–90, 92.
   See Vignettes and references to
   vignettes: Compatibility with
   Standards-Based Teaching;
   Vignettes and references to
   vignettes: Design Challenges;
   Vignettes and references to
   vignettes: Writing Dialogue

Hill, K. G., 41
Holistic rubrics, 104
Howard County Public School System, 95
Howe, A., 34
Hwang, J., 1, 10

Implicit Attitudes Test, 31
Implicit beliefs about creativity, 9–10
Improvement-potential perception, 52
Individual growth, 2–3
Initiate, Respond, Evaluate (IRE), 84
Inspiration, 30–31
Integrating sources, 75
Interacting with professionals, 30
Interest and motivation, 47
Internal creativity, 22
Intrinsic motivation. *See also* Vignettes
    and references to vignettes: Verb
    Tense; Vignettes and references to
    vignettes: Writing Dialogue
    importance, 41–44, 106
    and lessons, 76–78
    protecting/supporting, 45–51
    and writing, 73
Invented spelling, 23
Investment Theory of Creativity, 28
IRE (Initiate, Respond, Evaluate), 84
Iyengar, S. S., 50

Janusian thinking, 92
Jarvin, L., 29–30, 102, 105
Jindal-Snape, D., 34

Kamdar, D., 31
Kaufman, J. C., 1, 3, 5–6, 9, 21–22,
    27–30, 33, 36, 40, 45–46, 50, 60,
    101–102, 106
Khazanchi, S., 43
Kirschner, P. A., 100
Knowledge of creativity, 33
Kruglanski, A. W., 42
Kyllonen, P. C., 50

Language conventions, 75
Language standards, 70

Leal, Gabriel (student), 27
Learning conditions, 100
Legendary creativity. *See* Big-C creativity
Lepper, M. R., 42, 44, 50
Lesson-generating process, 94–95
Levels of creativity, 22–29, 35
Levenson, E., 84
Lewis, M., 52
Listening to students, 24
Little-c creativity, 25–26
Lofing, N., 27
Long-term motivation, 58–59
Lubart, T. I., 28

Maehr, M. L., 45
MAE (means to another end) principle, 100
Makel, M. C., 102
Maria (student), 28
Mathematics
    content domains of, 91–92, 94
    modeling, 79–80, 85–87, 89
    pattern recognition, 90
    precision, 86, 90, 95–97
    problem solving, 82–84, 88
    quantitative reasoning, 88
    reasoning, 79–81
    rubric for, 105
    standards, 15–16
    tools use, 85–87, 89–90, 95–97
Mathematics standards. *See* Common
    Core State Standards: math
McMaken, J., 1, 10
McNeil, L. M., 11
Meaning in context, 55–56
Means to another end (MAE) principle, 100
Mecklenburg, A. C., 43
Medeiros, K. W., 92
Mehan, H., 26, 84
Melwani, S., 31
Memorization, 14–16, 18
Mertler, C. A., 104–105
Middle school, 65, 89–92. *See* Vignettes
    and references to vignettes:
    Applying Math Knowledge

Midgley, C., 44–45
Mini-c creativity, 22–25, 35, 107
Minority students, 11
Modeling with mathematics, 79–80,
    85–87, 89
Morphological Synthesis, 103–104
Motivation, 39–45, 52–54. *See also*
    Extrinsic motivation; Intrinsic
    motivation
Mowrer-Reynolds, E., 32
Mueller, J. S., 31
Multiple solutions, 84–85, 95–96
Mumford, M. D., 92
Museum activity, 93

Narrative techniques, 56–57
Narrow focus of curriculum, 11
National Governors Association Center
    for Best Practices. *See* NGACPB
    (National Governors Association
    Center for Best Practices)
Newman, J. L., 77
New situations vignette, 81–85
News stories and editorials vignette,
    63–65, 74–75
New York Times, 63–64
NGACPB (National Governors
    Association Center for Best
    Practices), 10, 15–17, 40, 43,
    56–57, 63–66, 68–71, 74–75, 80,
    82, 86, 88, 92, 94, 96
Niu, W., 83
Nonevaluation, 77
Nongrading, 72, 77

Opposite ideas, 92
Options and motivation, 50–51
Oral, G., 32
Orangeworms, 27
Originality, 21, 24, 35
Other-oriented motivation, 43
Overpraising, 30

Paley, V. G., 24
Partlow, P. J., 92
Pattern recognition, 90

Permanence-avoidant orientation, 45
Personal creativity. *See* Mini-c creativity
Personal insights, 22–23
Personal perspective, 22–24
Pierce, W., 43
Pistachios, 27
Pizza restaurant vignette, 79–80
Plucker, J. A., 6, 21, 102
Poetry writing, 55–56
Point of view, 72, 75
Porter, A., 1, 10
Practice, 26
Practicing skills, 16
Praise, 30, 76–77, 106
Precision, 86, 90, 95–97
Prescription versus guidance, 18–19
Pressure on teachers, 11–12
Pretz, J. E., 6, 106
Principled use of techniques, 99
Prior knowledge, 22, 74, 77
Problem solving, 14–15, 82–84, 88
Pro-c creativity, 26
Professional creativity. *See* Pro-c
    creativity
Project duration, 94–95

Quantitative reasoning, 88

Reading literature, 15
Reading standards, 67–68, 71
Realistic application/context, 79–80,
    85–87, 95–97
Reasoning and motivation, 49–50
Reeve, J. M., 49–51
Reiter-Palmon, R., 13
Repeated reasoning, 90–91
Repetition, 16
Reworking lessons, 92–93
Rhodes, M., 21
Risk taking, 23, 58–59, 77
"Road Not Taken, The," 55, 71
Robins, R. W., 52
Robinson, E. J., 13
Rosiek, J., 51
Rothenberg, A., 92
Rubrics, 102–106

Runco, M. A., 3
Ryan, R. M., 41, 43, 48–51

Saddler, B., 102
Sammy vignette, 20–21, 33–34
SCAMPER (Substitute, Combine,
    Adapt, Modify, Put to Another
    Use, Eliminate, Reverse), 104
Schmidt, H. G., 100
Schulten, K., 63
Science class vignette, 20–21
Self-directed learning, 48–49
Self-knowledge, 22, 33
Self-oriented motivation, 43
Seo, C., 22–23, 25
Shame, 52
Shanock, L., 43
Sharing creative ideas, 25–26, 35,
    79–80, 85
Shepard, L. A., 10
Short-term motivation, 58–59
Silliness, 16–17, 63
Simonton, D. K., 5, 21, 28
Skill-building, 57–59, 73
Smith, S. M., 92
Social appropriateness, 21
Social comparison of students, 45
Social studies example, 25, 63–65
Solutions from creative process, 14–15
Speaker's point of view, 75
Speaking and listening standards, 69–70
Standardized testing, 2
Standards for Mathematical Content
    (MC), 91–97
Standards for Mathematical Practice
    (MP), 87–97
"Standards in Your State," 1
Sternberg, R. J., 6, 9, 26, 28–30, 82,
    102, 105–106
Stifling of creativity, 39–40, 52
Strauss, V., 1, 10
Structure discernment, 90
Student autonomy, 49, 51
Student perspectives, 50
Substantive feedback, 24–25

Substitute, Combine, Adapt, Modify,
    Put to Another Use, Eliminate,
    Reverse (SCAMPER), 104
Sullivan, M. W., 52
Supportive feedback, 24–25
Suppression of creativity, 39–40, 52
Sweller, J., 100
Synergism, 4

Tan, M., 29–30, 102, 105
Task appropriateness, 21, 24
Taylor, I. A., 106
Teaching creativity, 98–101
Te Winkel, W. W. R., 100
Tighe, E. M., 41
Time constraints, 44–45
Tolerance for ambiguity, 31
Tomato garden activity, 96–97
Tools use, 85–87, 89–90, 95–97
Torrance, E. P., 32
Toxic spill lesson example, 95–96
Tracy, J. L., 52
Transferring knowledge, 81–85

Universal creative potential, 18
Unlegislated standards, 10

Van der Molen, H. T., 100
Vignettes and references to vignettes
    Applying Math Knowledge, 81–85
    Cold Facts?, 20, 23
    "Creativity Time"?, 8–9
    Design Challenges, 85–87
    Divergent Thinking, 60–63, 73–74
    Fact, Opinion, and Reasoned
        Judgment, 63–65, 74–75
    Is Creativity Compatible with
        Standards-Based Teaching?, 8–9
    Mathematical Permutations and
        Combinations, 79–80
    Math Motorcycles, 38, 44–45
    Meanings of Words, 55–60, 71
    Okay to Stifle Creativity?, 20–21,
        33–34
    Reading Ratatouille, 39, 41–42

Verb Tense and Storytelling, 65–66, 75
Writing Dialogue, 56–57, 72–73
Vygotsky, L. S., 22

Walters, A. M., 50
Ward, T. B., 92
Westby, E. L., 31
Wijnen, W. H. F. W., 100
Work and creativity, 19

Writing standards, 68–69

Yang, R., 1, 10

Zbikowski, S. M., 57
Zeevi, G., 42
Zhou, J. Z., 83
Zwicky, F., 103
Zwicky Box, 103–104

About the Authors

Ronald A. Beghetto is an associate professor of educational psychology at the University of Connecticut. Prior to joining the faculty at UConn, he served as the College of Education's associate dean for academic affairs and associate professor of education studies at the University of Oregon. Dr. Beghetto earned his PhD in educational psychology from Indiana University. His research focuses on creativity in educational settings, and he has extensive experience providing professional development to educators with the goal of supporting creative teaching, learning, and assessment in K–12 and higher-education settings. Dr. Beghetto has published numerous books, scholarly articles, and book chapters on classroom creativity. He is the editor-in-chief for the _Journal of Creative Behavior_ and serves as an associate editor for the _International Journal of Creativity and Problem Solving_. Dr. Beghetto is a fellow of the American Psychological Association and the Society for the Psychology of Aesthetics, Creativity and the Arts (Div. 10, APA). He has received numerous awards for his research and teaching.

James C. Kaufman is a professor of educational psychology at the Neag School of Education at the University of Connecticut. An internationally recognized leader in the field of creativity, he is the author/editor of 30 books, including _Creativity 101_ and the _Cambridge Handbook of Creativity_, as well as more than 200 papers. Kaufman is the past president of American Psychological Association's Division 10, which is devoted to creativity and aesthetics. He is the founding co-editor of _Psychology of Popular Media Culture_ and co-founded _Psychology of Aesthetics, Creativity, and the Arts_, both published by APA. He has won numerous awards, including the Torrance Award from the National Association for Gifted Children, the Berlyne and Farnsworth Awards from APA, and Mensa's research award.

John Baer is a professor of educational psychology at Rider University. His research on the development of creativity and his teaching have both won national awards, including the American Psychological Association's Berlyne Prize and the National Conference on College Teaching and Learning's Award for Innovative Excellence. His books include _Being Creative_

Inside and Outside the Classroom; Creativity and Divergent Thinking: A Task-Specific Approach; Creative Teachers, Creative Students; Creativity Across Domains: Faces of the Muse; Reason and Creativity in Development; Are We Free? Psychology and Free Will; and *Essentials of Creativity Assessment.* He has been a teacher and program director in gifted education and served as a regional director in the Odyssey of the Mind creative problem-solving program.